WITHDRAWN

WITHDRAWN

MARATHON 16

BY THE SAME AUTHORS

Games Analysts Play

MARTIN SHEPARD, M.D.

and MARJORIE LEE

Marathon 16

G. P. PUTNAM'S SONS

NEW YORK

CARL A. RUDISILL LIBRARY
LENOIR RHYNE COLLEGE

Copyright © 1970 by Martin Shepard and Marjorie Lee. All rights reserved.
This book, or parts thereof, must not be reproduced in any form without per-
mission. Published simultaneously in Canada by Longmans Canada Limited,
Toronto.

Library of Congress Catalog Card Number: 71–118075

PRINTED IN THE UNITED STATES OF AMERICA

361.4
Sh4m

74733

July, 1971

For our ten participants,
without whom ...

Thanks are due the following group leaders who have most influenced me: Aaron Stein, Albert Ellis, Jon Geis, Fritz Perls, Bill Schutz, and Stuart and Sarah Miller

M. S.

My gratitude for special help goes to Robert S. Lee, Sr., John Post Lee, Steven Merriam Lee, Elizabeth Kilraine, Anne Tiffany, Hannah Lees, and Max Gartenberg

M. L.

Introduction

The purpose of this book is to give the essence, the guts, of an actual marathon encounter as it was experienced by ten participants within an unbroken time span of sixteen hours.

Over the last several years, psychologically oriented group sessions have expanded in concept and intent. Whereas once they were conducted to treat neurotic individuals for an hour or two each week, they are now being used to deal with the so-called "normal" person who may simply wish to get a bit more out of life; and while traditional Freudian techniques have, thus far, stressed the analysis and "talking out" of difficulties in living, encounter methods offer participants a chance for *new experiences.* Growth is seen as learning new ways of relating rather than being limited to the dissection of old patterns of behavior.

This new concept of group treatment requires a more extended period of time than hourly sessions in order to make its impact felt. "Workshops" are often held over weekends, or for full weeks, in settings far removed from the distractions of familiar environments; or in nonstop marathons lasting anywhere from ten to thirty hours. It is this latter type of session which forms the basis of this book.

Our ten participants were, for the most part, "cocktail party" acquaintances of Martin Shepard and were, by and large, unknown to each other. Dr. Shepard spoke randomly with twenty people in the three weeks prior to the enactment of *Marathon 16,* asking if they would trade this free experience in return for the use of their ensuing material for book purposes. Half of those he contacted were agreeable to the arrangement.

The dialogue, the interactions, and the response material of Part I are presented as recorded on tape, with deletions of several rambling and cumbersome verbal productions which were found to be destructive to readability. The only pertinent detail to be withheld from publication is the identification of the participants by their real names. The aliases, written on tags and worn throughout the clothed sessions, were those chosen by the participants themselves. How and why each one selected his particular pseudonym becomes apparent in a later portion of the marathon.

Dr. Shepard, in effect the eleventh participant, is referred to as *M* and, in certain instances, as *Marty*. *Marjorie* signifies Marjorie Lee, co-author of this book, whose role at the marathon was that of observer and the taker of expositive notes in order to report visual aspects of action and expression, precisely as descriptions and stage directions appear in a written presentation of a theatrical play. It should be understood, however, that total nonparticipation, total objectivity, in such emotional and compelling circumstances is humanly impossible. The phenomenology of Mrs. Lee's involvement is given in Part II: "Marathon Observed."

M. S.

M. L.

August, 1969

Contents

Acknowledgments   6

Introduction   7

Dramatis Personae   11

The Set   11

PART ONE: THE MARATHON

Act 1: First Impressions   15

     SCENE 1: FRIEND OR FOE   15

     SCENE 2: REACTIONS   36

Act 2: The Most Distressing Thing   39

Act 3: The Most Shameful Thing   51

     SCENE 1: SEXUAL SHAMES   51

     SCENE 2: BERNARD'S HANG-UP   67

     SCENE 3: SMALLER BUGGINGS   75

     SCENE 4: LITTLE PRINCE'S FREAK-OUT   77

     SCENE 5: KARI'S TRIP   84

     SCENE 6: LITTLE PRINCE RETURNS   92

Act 4: The Dominant-Passive Game   100

     SCENE 1: THE LINEUP   100

     SCENE 2: DISCUSSION   101

Act 5: Personal Ratings   108

     SCENE 1: BERNARD'S OBNOXIOUSNESS   108

     SCENE 2: HOW SEXY AM I?   113

Act 6: Take a Risk   118
    SCENE 1: A BUILDUP OF COURAGE   118
    SCENE 2: BERNARD'S NORMALCY   121
    SCENE 3: YAEL'S TRIP   126
    SCENE 4: THE FIGHT   139
    SCENE 5: SARAH'S LONELINESS   153

Act 7: Love Relationships   160

Act 8: Nudity   176
    SCENE 1: UNDRESSING   176
    SCENE 2: BODY EVALUATIONS   184
    SCENE 3: TAKE A WALK   194
    SCENE 4: THE FORCING OF PHILIP   198
    SCENE 5: THE BODY CHESS GAME   202
    SCENE 6: THE QUICK TURN-ON   207
    SCENE 7: HELP SOMEONE   212
    SCENE 8: HE LOVES ME NOT   216
    SCENE 9: HE LOVES ME   223
    SCENE 10: DISCUSSION   231

Act 9: The Windup   232
    SCENE 1: WHAT'S IN A NAME?   232
    SCENE 2: WHAT DO YOU DO?   236
    SCENE 3: ANYONE WALKING OVER TO BROADWAY?   239

PART TWO: EVALUATION

1. Marathon Observed • *Marjorie Lee*   242
2. Commentary • *Martin Shepard, M.D.*   249

DRAMATIS PERSONAE

M	*a male psychiatrist of 34, leader of the marathon*
LITTLE PRINCE	*a female Flower Child of 21*
SARAH	*an attractive woman of 39*
YAEL	*a German Jewess of 41*
JANE	*a girl of 28*
KARI OLSEN	*a Norwegian girl of 29*
SHERSHONSKY	*a quiet man of 39*
BOB	*an equally quiet man of 27*
ROBERT LEA	*a not-so-quiet man of 35*
PHILIP	*a male Hippie of 18*
BERNARD SCHLOSSBERG	*a strong man of 35, built for wrestling*
MARJORIE	*a woman of 48: co-author and observer; pre-ordained nonparticipant*

Note: Further description of these "characters" will appear in context.

Time: From 10 A.M., June 21, 1969, through 2 A.M., June 22, 1969

Place: The office of Dr. Martin Shepard, 12 West 96th Street, New York City

It is a rather small room, one belonging to an apartment of other offices, bathrooms, and a kitchen, led into by a foyer and a long hall. The décor, unlike that of the offices of classical, or traditional, psychiatrists and psychoanalysts, is casual and haphazard. On one wall there is a child's poster-paint creation, largely "primitive" and red; on another, an undisciplined nonobjective oil in black, white, and grays. There are two windows, shuttered but uncurtained, which represent the city in terms of much soot and little view. An assortment of questionable plants in varied pots has been removed to another room in order to make space for, and to facilitate possible action on the part of, participants. Books fill bracketed wall shelves. The large desk, set beneath an array of thumbtacked cartoons, notes, and memorabilia, is piled high with papers, pamphlets, pens, pencils, and a typewriter. The furniture is of modern Danish persuasion; the colors are brown, beige, and orange. The analytic couch has been joined by another, borrowed from the waiting room, to allow for sufficient sitting space. The floor is carpeted, wall to wall, and looks comfortable. There is no evidence at all of framed medical and psychiatric degrees. In spite of the general confusion, it is a room in which one is encouraged to feel free and very, very much at ease.

PART ONE

THE MARATHON

Act 1: First Impressions

SCENE 1: FRIEND OR FOE

The participants have arrived, each alone, and filled in personal information blanks. They have also signed legal releases for the use, in book and/or movie form, of all verbalized and performed material resulting in and from the marathon. To their surprise, each one has been handed a dollar bill.

Upon arrival, they were instructed to keep totally silent, remove their shoes, and choose a new name to be written on a tag and pasted to their clothing. Having left their shoes and their old identities in the waiting room, they now sit, uncommunicating, in M's office.

Settled adjacently on couches and chairs are Bob, Shershonsky, Yael, Sarah, Bernard, Jane, Little Prince, Philip, Robert Lea, and M. Kari prefers to sit on the floor, against the wall near M's chair, as if in partial hiding. Marjorie sits, Turk fashion, on the hall floor, just beyond the open office door, in full view and hearing of the proceedings.

There is a feeling of both tension and embarrassment in the silence. Occasionally a throat is cleared. Bob's smile remains constant; Yael's flickers on and off. The rest look down at their hands in their laps or cast somewhat fur-

tive glances at their fellow participants. As the moments pass, courage is gained, and the glances turn to longer stares of assessment.

M has entered. He is wearing shorts, a sport shirt, and sandals and exudes an air of casual but strong confidence. He is thirty-four, tall, clean-shaven, and good-looking in a dark, full-blooded way.

M: First, I want to thank you all for coming down here; and second, I want to explain a couple of ground rules. There's an ice box full of sodas in the back. You may help yourself to them as you like. We'll be meeting for a long time, and, if you like, there'll be meals. You can, at any time, stay outside alone. There are two other offices, the doors of which are both open. If you want to go and talk with any other person, it's got to be done within a five-minute period, and when you come back you've got to tell us what went on between you and the other person. *(He lifts one sandaled foot up to his chair, sprawling open-legged and comfortably.)* I think you'll all have an interesting time if you'll try to say what you're feeling. Don't sit on it in an attempt to be nice, polite, or spare somebody's feelings. Do what you feel like doing, but when you have an impulse to do something, remember you're all responsible adults. We're going to go through a number of procedures, but we can depart from them at any point if anybody has something they want to say. I'm asking you not to smoke because I think people usually take cigarettes when they're tense about something. I think you'll be better off figuring out what's making you tense and seeing if you can talk about it, or experience it. Besides, the room is quite small and if you smoke it's going to be uncomfortable for a lot of us. The reason I've asked you to start off with silence, aside from getting in touch with your own feelings, is that I'd like to begin with the First Impression Game. And for that, I'd like each of you to stand up in the center of the room, and, one by one, people will come over and give their first impressions of you. I'd like you to notice how much you can know about a person without listening to him—just from your sense of feel, sight, touch, and smell. See how they stand, what their posture's like, what they do with their hands, how their necks and chins are set, what their faces feel like, what their muscles feel like. Sniff them. Taste them. Anything but talk with them. And as you're examining them, run down your impressions out loud for us. This is Marjorie Lee, by the way. She's going to be here writing and describing what goes on. She won't be participating. My name, henceforth, will be *M*.

Bob

Bob is the first to offer himself for examination. He was also the first to arrive but went immediately to the hall bathroom before entering the office. He has been sitting quietly with a shy half-smile on his face. He is twenty-seven, brown-eyed, and wears a short-sleeved button-down white shirt, loose brown pants, and a neatly trimmed short beard.

Little Prince rises from the couch and approaches him. She is twenty-one, of medium height, and wears a flowered, floor-length skirt with a matching African tie-bra which leaves her middle bare. Her red-blond hair reaches beyond her shoulders, and her glasses are round, metal-framed, and of the lastest "granny" style. Behind them, her eyes are green. Her face has a rather ordinary prettiness, but her body, beneath the scant clothing, suggests perfection. She takes Bob's hands in hers, then feels his arms, and begins to speak in a soft, breathy, and almost romantic tone.

LITTLE PRINCE: You blink a lot . . . You have a smile that's almost constantly there, but a little stiff. I think you're a very

honest, open person, and I enjoy the idea that you got up
first to volunteer for this. Your muscles are a little tense . . .
not much. But they're soft. And strong, though. (*She touches
his hair; feels it, sniffs it.*) It's cut short. It has something in
it, but it doesn't detract from it too much. Your smile gets
better every time I look at you. I admire soft things very
much. . . .

> *There is general laughter.*
>
> *Bernard offers to examine Bob next. He is a handsome
> thirty-five-year-old man, broad, powerfully built, with
> well-chiseled features and a neat beard. He wears a pink
> short-sleeved shirt and trousers which are extremely, al-
> most bizarrely, tight. He begins his evaluation from his
> seat on the couch.*

BERNARD: You seem like a very nice guy. Not an aggressive, tough
kind of person. I'm almost wondering whether this is a reflection of weakness or not. I'm suspicious.

M: You want to stand up?

BERNARD (*rising, approaching Bob*): You look slightly anxious.
And like some typical person you see in the advertisements.
A very average build, an average way of standing. I don't
feel the necessity to pinch you or push you because I . . .
uh . . . uh . . . because I get the feeling of what you're like.

> *Yael arises and goes toward Bob. She is a diminutive
> woman of forty-one, surely under five feet tall. Her short
> dark hair fits her head like a curly cap. Her features are
> small and sharp, particularly the eyes, under full, un-
> plucked eyebrows, which peer out like tiny, shiny black
> buttons. Her blue slacks and multi-colored blouse give
> her a look of compactness. She is half gremlin, half bird,
> a woman whose intelligence and no-nonsense directness
> are immediately to be reckoned with. There is charm in
> her German accent and in her speech, which is filled
> with foreign inversions of grammar.*

YAEL: I don't have anything to add except that to me you represent many types that I have seen before, and I was thinking that maybe you were Arabic or Israeli. I like you.

Shershonsky rises and approaches Bob. He is a quiet man of thirty-nine with a look of gentleness. He is blue-eyed and moustached and wears khaki chino pants and a blue work shirt.

SHERSHONSKY: When I first came into the room I saw you sitting there and there was something . . . uh, sort of gentle. Uh . . . when I heard Bernard describe you as . . . as weak, I, uh, thought of somehow wanting to take your side. I don't think you're a weak guy. You're a guy who doesn't come on strong, but who could take care of himself. . . . Good vibrations. (*He chuckles.*)

Sarah takes her turn with Bob. She is thirty-nine, and wears white slacks and a brown Paisley blouse with long sleeves. Her hair is dark and her eyes incredibly blue. If she is a WASP, and that cannot yet be known, she exudes the most attractive qualities of that sometimes-questionable stereotype: a clean, uncosmeticized face; poise; "breeding"; and a voice quietly firm and deep. She, like Yael, seems obviously intelligent to a superior degree, but in a different way: Sarah is less sharp, perhaps more patient.

SARAH: I get the feeling you're kind of a responsible person because you got up first . . . also protective, by the way you did it, so that other people didn't have to. I get a feeling you're anxious, but probably not as anxious as I am.

Jane goes to Bob. She is a conventionally good-looking girl of twenty-eight with short light hair and blue eyes. She wears a short-sleeved chenille shirt and tight blue jeans which give her a look of firm, athletic healthiness.

JANE: You seem very eager to please. Your smile . . . I don't think that's a weakness thing, I think it's just that you're very pli-

able and take a lot of responsibility, and if somebody wanted
to—they could probably shit on you.

*Robert Lea goes to Bob next. He is thirty-five, dark, of
medium height. His body seems strong and slightly
squared off in a white shirt and jeans. His beard is neat,
his face firm, his stance sure; and his chin leads with a
touch of confident aggressivity. The voice and speech,
New York-accented, carry a subtle underlay of a Bronx or
Brooklyn upbringing; but there is an educated intellec-
tuality in his delivery which bespeaks a breakaway from
earlier limitations and puts him into that large group of
New Yorkers in which brightness and a good mind are
the entrance tickets to all "classes." His impressions of
Bob match those of the others: nice, likable, eager to
please.*

*Philip, eighteen, is our boy Hippie: tall, thin, bearded,
and long-haired, wearing a long-sleeved blue shirt and
jeans. His boots were removed upon entering. In his large-
nosed face, in his enormous brown eyes, there is the look
of saintliness so coveted by many youths today. His hair,
if clean, does not appear to be; nor is it thoroughly
combed. He approaches Bob with a slow but graceful
gait.*

PHILIP: I notice you slouch a lot, and, uh, it makes such a difference when you stand up because you're probably five-
eleven, five-ten. . . .

BOB: Five-eight.

PHILIP: Well, if you stood up you'd be five-ten. (*General laughter.*)

*It is now Kari's turn to do Bob. She is a large, blond
Norwegian of twenty-nine, wearing a green-striped one-
piece jump suit. Her accent and intonation are subtly
reminiscent of Ingrid Bergman's.*

KARI: I do feel . . . I sense an anxiousness. . . . I don't feel that your body is really involved or that it has a life of its own. I wouldn't use "kindness" or any of those words. . . . An instinct, uh . . . something that goes against what your daily life is . . . (*It becomes apparent that while Kari feels deeply, she must work hard to translate her feelings into thoughts and her thoughts into words.*)

Robert Lea

Bernard is the first to examine Robert Lea.

BERNARD: I'm always, uh, initially suspicious of people with beards. You seem like a pretty straight guy, though; pretty forthright, and you have a friendly, intelligent face. I'm not put off as I frequently am by people with beards. (*We see that Bernard, himself bearded, is impervious to the humor in his comments. He is in dead earnest about this, and about himself.*)

SHERSHONSKY: Well, the impression that I get is you're kind of . . . uh . . . aggressive and authoritarian. That may come out of *me.*

SARAH: There's solidity about you, but more in the physical sense. (*She goes on to describe Robert Lea as the others have: straightforwardness, competence; and adds that he does feel comfortable about his body, with very little show of tenseness except in his fingers.*)

YAEL: I feel more comfortable when you smile, and I would like to take the beard off, but I have nothing against beards in general.

BOB: I get the impression that part of you is just a façade—the aggressiveness, the harshness. Once you're able to get past this barrier, this façade . . . um . . . I think it would be possible to set up a very warm, close relationship.

Jane and Philip both agree with what has already been said about Robert Lea; Jane adds that she feels she has met him somewhere before, at a party.

LITTLE PRINCE (*breathily, poetically*): You have a very distinct profile, and this enchanting moustache. . . . The first thing that came into my mind was Henri Bergson . . . skeptical . . . brilliant type of scientist of some sort. The façade . . . I would call it an image you think maybe you have to carry out. And what it takes to put it away is a moment, maybe a very simple, feeling moment. . . . And your voice is surprisingly soft. I thought it was going to bellow out of your stomach! (*She feels his shoulders and muscles.*) You're solid! Yah! (*General laughter.*)

Sarah

BERNARD: You have a sort of motherly . . . uh . . . you seem very mature. . . .

M: Bernard, can you take your hands out of your pockets? See if you can turn on other than visually. (*Bernard puts his hands behind his back.*) No, behind your back is no better than in your pockets.

BERNARD: I feel a little inhibited about touching, you know. I feel that later I might . . . Uh . . . so that's the first thing: this very mature woman. The sort of person I would see at Martha's Vineyard. Slightly WASP'y, very assured . . .

YAEL: It certainly was very good when I saw you coming in here, because I thought to myself, "My goodness, I'm the only one over thirty!" I tried to place you somewhere, maybe in Europe or something, to know where you come from and who you are and how you got here. I . . . get a good feeling. (*Yael's accent is less self-conscious now: there is a short, clipped ring to it.*)

> *Little Prince evaluates Sarah with almost the same breathy romanticness that she uses with the men. She finds Sarah beautiful, sympathetic, and warm and says that she would like to paint a picture of her looking out of a window.*

Kari, Robert Lea, Shershonsky, and Bob all concur about Sarah's beauty, repose, and warmth. Special praise is given to the blueness of her eyes. Philip notes the dark shadows beneath them.

M: Philip, do you want to touch her, feel her?

Philip declines the invitation and sits down.

Yael

LITTLE PRINCE: Yael, I think you're absolutely precious! The most joyful face! But that doesn't mean you haven't suffered. It's like Malcolm Boyd said: "If I'm gonna die, I'm gonna die laughing." . . . And you have these tiny, little eyes that I just want to peer right into! I think you're one of these nitty-gritty grass-roots persons . . . and I just . . . I just take so much delight in watching you!

Shershonsky, Robert Lea, Kari, and Bob all amplify Little Prince's impressions. They find Yael tiny but strong; vital, immediate. They imagine her as working with dedication on a kibbutz. They are struck by the force which seems to lie behind her smallness.

BERNARD: I have a very . . . visceral reaction. You're very different-looking from most people. Pixie-ish, gnomelike . . .

M: Bernard, I can respect your feeling that you don't know people well enough to touch them, but if that's an inhibition you're up-tight about, you might take a chance and see what the experience is like.

BERNARD (*hesitantly touching Yael's arms and shoulders*): I . . . uh . . . don't have an overwhelming desire to handle you. The thing that impressed me first was that you've got an enormous amount of confidence despite the fact that you're, you know, shorter than most people.

Philip approaches her.

YAEL (*nervously*): I wish I had pockets!

PHILIP: At first I didn't notice you. Then when you began to speak, it started me on the road to endearment.

JANE: Your eyes are amazing, alive. And when you feel happy you're really happy, and when you're sad you're really sad. You're alive. You . . . you live, every moment.

Shershonsky

KARI: I truly feel that you would like to evaluate people in a nice way. I get good vibrations from you. You are what I would call a Nice Guy. (*General laughter.*)

M: Kari, you're also someone who judges people from a distance. Do you want to try it a different way?

KARI: No. No . . . uh . . . right now I have a lot of feelings and by touching . . . it wouldn't add at this point. Maybe I would like to see how he would express himself physically, aggressively. That body just hasn't made up its mind, taken a stand, even towards itself. . . .

M: Do you want to wrestle with him?

KARI: No.

> *Robert Lea suggests that Shershonsky, while a pleasant person, represses his aggression in the fear that he will hurt people, or, possibly, himself.*
>
> *Sarah tells Shershonsky that he is a pleasant and handsome man and that she would like to hand-wrestle with him. They stretch out on the floor, on their stomachs, and begin. There are a few grunts. Then Shershonsky pins Sarah's arm down.*
>
> *Little Prince finds Shershonsky physically "beautiful" and "lovely." She says that she would like to "be with" him so that she might "hear" his thoughts.*
>
> *Yael states that it is incomprehensible to her that Shershonsky should wrestle with Sarah when he could have put his arms around her instead.*
>
> *M lifts Yael up and places her on a chair so that she can*

*evaluate Shershonsky from a new vantage point. Yael tells
how things look different now.*

*Bob's evaluation of Shershonsky echoes those of the
other participants: a nice guy who, for some reason, holds
back his inner aggressivity.*

BERNARD: I can't give an initial impression of you, Shershonsky,
because I've met you before. You look like a kind of hung-up
guy. I get the feeling you try to avoid too intimate contact
with people.

M: Bernard, see if you can allow yourself to use your hands. See
how he feels, lift his arms.

*Bernard does so; then sits down without further com-
ment.*

Jane goes to Shershonsky and hugs him warmly.

JANE: When I did that, you sort of stiffened and pulled away.
You hang back. You're afraid somebody's going to get you.

Kari

*Little Prince evaluates Kari first. She touches her hands
and her hair, then speaks so softly and breathlessly that
she can hardly be heard.*

LITTLE PRINCE: I really like you. I'd like to talk to you sometime. I don't quite understand some of the thoughts you put
out. Maybe we just don't think in the same patterns. Your
hands are so pretty, and your eyes have a sort of saddish curve
to them. . . .

ROBERT LEA (*touching Kari's arm*): You seem very well assured
of yourself, but perhaps you don't really put yourself to the
test to see if you would be victorious or defeated in certain
situations.

PHILIP: I think when you talk things come out without censor-
ship. Open . . . And I think you're very sexy.

M: Do you want to feel her?

PHILIP: I don't think you should encourage it at this point. I mean, we're going to be here for a long time. For me, when I touch, I would like to touch unencouraged.

JANE: I don't know whether you're open or not, but the feeling I get from you is sort of cold and distant.

SHERSHONSKY: Uh . . . very trim, like athletically . . . physically capable. (*He feels her shoulders.*) Strong, really solid. I have the impression that you're the sort of person who will move into a situation very strongly, but perhaps you aren't really as sure as you think you are about a lot of things. At first I kind of disliked you because you were kind of assertive, and I have a sort of thing about people who are kind of assertive. But then it kind of changed. . . .

> Bernard lifts Kari to ascertain her weight. Then he speaks of her "peasant, physical qualities."
> M lifts Yael to a chair for her evaluation of Kari.

M (*to Yael*): It's a very rare experience for you. View the world as a six-footer.

YAEL (*to Kari*): I'm especially fascinated with your face when you get these three little lines, frowning, when you say something to people. Especially when you mentioned the division of mind and body. I think you've got a beautiful build, and . . . and the uh-other thing I thought was that if only I could wear a thing like that thing you're wearing. If I had the courage! I . . . I . . . I feel also a little bit of anxiousness in . . . in your eyes, as if you're worried what is going to happen and what will people say and how will they react.

> M asks Yael to step down from the chair and give another impression from her normal height.

YAEL: It's very hard, very hard because I have never seen you like that, from high up, only sitting. You have very beautiful eyes, but I still see that worry a little bit. And the other thing I was thinking is "What-what-what is she doing in real life, and how does she manage?" I'll find out!

M: If we can avoid talking about what we do in real life till the end it will be more useful in that people won't fit you into slots as easily, as be intimidated as easily.

BERNARD: Why don't we make it a game, like eight hours from now we can try to guess.

M: That seems like a good idea. Maybe we'll wrap it up that way.

The focus goes back to Kari, as Sarah stands up to evaluate her.

SARAH: When I first came in I was so fascinated by you. And I think maybe that's because you look so Scandinavian. All my stereotypes about Scandinavians are sort of healthy, athletic, competent, reserved, and all sorts of other mythical aspects from the Ingmar Bergman movies. But the impression I get since you started to talk is of someone who really wants to cut through all the crap. You'll say something straightforward even if it's not totally kind.

Bob endorses the group's impressions of Kari but adds that she seems scared and mistrustful.

Little Prince

Little Prince takes the floor, and Yael is the first to approach her.

YAEL: First of all, I thought that you really had courage of wearing whatever you felt like wearing. I think that was very beautiful. And before you even talked, I said to myself, "My goodness, what gorgeous hair!" The other thing that fascinates me is that you seem to, uh . . . to know a lot. I mean, you mentioned Henri Bergson, and all kind of things. I'm quite fascinated with that . . . uh . . . softness in you when you talk to people. It doesn't matter if you talk to women or talk to men. You have that same type of very sensual, very sexual kind of feeling. It's lovely.

BERNARD (*stepping up to Little Prince*): I've been very anxious to do you. (*There is a general chorus of exclamations and peals of laughter.*)

M: Do her how?

BERNARD: I'll do her *my* way.

M: What is your way?

BERNARD: Obviously, the first impression I got is: What's she doing in this kooky outfit? I think you're somebody who's conscious of making some kind of impression on people; you like to be reacted to. The strongest quality that comes across to me is of intense femininity. You have, uh . . . uh . . . all the right hormones. A good dose.

> *Little Prince is pleased by this. She kneels down before Bernard. Bernard smells her arm. Her stomach and bare middle move up and down with her sudden depth of breathing.*

BOB: I like your name, first of all. I think it's very, very appropriate.

M: "Little Prince"? That's a *man*.

BOB: I know, but in terms of what it stands for, I thought that would be obvious. You're warm. I thought you'd be freezing. I . . . I liked the way you just came in at first and sat down and got into this plastic, kind of relaxed position. The impression I got was not so much of femininity as of warmth. You relate to both men and women in a very close warm way.

YAEL: Did you walk in the streets in those clothes?

LITTLE PRINCE: Yes.

ROBERT LEA: Wild, how wild!

> *Little Prince laughs breathily.*
>
> *Kari evaluates Little Prince in rather vague, abstract terms and speaks of her feelings of "estrangement" from her.*

ROBERT LEA: There emanates from you a very, very warm, sensual, sexual quality. I don't want to touch you because I could eat you up right this minute. You really dig rapping with people, where you can elevate your ideas and the communication between you and someone else. Almost I would define it as a sort of cerebral orgasm.

SHERSHONSKY: You look like someone who might perhaps be a dancer. And then I was kind of surprised at the way you were able to observe people and discuss them. Then I wondered if the verbal, intellectual part and the belly-dancer part were really in accord.

> *Shershonsky goes on to say that Little Prince's intellectuality puts him off. He would rather relate to her physically.*

M: Relate physically.

> *Shershonsky touches her bare waist and then holds her close to him.*

SHERSHONSKY (*to M*): When you told me to do it, I developed a resentment, like "Who is he to tell me this kind of thing?"

M: Do you resent it while you're doing it?

SHERSHONSKY (*still holding Little Prince*): Well, it's nice, but I just resent the authority thing.

SARAH: I didn't understand the "Little Prince"—until just a minute ago when it occurred to me that that's from the Saint-Exupéry story. I found you were bringing out a lot of motherly feelings in me.

JANE: When I first saw you, I really hated you. I felt terribly jealous and terribly competitive. And when you talk you have this kind of actressy intensity. I thought, "Oh well, it's really phony and she's full of shit." But when I look at you, I really believe you. You have a beautiful face. I'd like to see you without your glasses. (*She removes the glasses to find that Little Prince has beautiful greenish eyes.*)

> *Philip rises and kisses Little Prince on the lips, then pauses.*

PHILIP: . . . I hope you didn't resent that, because you shouldn't be sore.

Jane

Little Prince begins by admitting a feeling of retaliative competition with Jane and an envy of Jane's having been able to hug Bob.

M: Hug her.

LITTLE PRINCE (*hugging Jane, as they both laugh*): Wow, you smell! Oh, it's beautiful! I really like you. You'd be just a great person to get to know!

YAEL (*appraising Jane*): Maybe that's my old age, but I didn't feel no competition or nothing. I have a feeling that . . . that here's a type of girl that I don't know anything about. Very, very strange to my whole frame of reference.

BERNARD: I also have difficulty classifying you right now. Uh, two things come through to me: One is bluntness; and I have a feeling you're a very good lay.

ROBERT LEA: I . . . I find that I remember you. Spoke to me one night. An economy of expression, a pretty face, and . . . um . . . a lovely neck, and, um . . . (*He trails off.*)

Sarah finds Jane straightforward and feels a kinship based on some strange, imaginary relationship in the past. Bob agrees with the general impression that Jane is open and straightforward and adds that she may also be shy. Kari picks up Sarah's feeling about a kinship in some distant past and adds that Jane could be very "nasty" if she put her mind to it.

SHERSHONSKY: I still can't quite figure you out . . . but I have a lot more good feelings about you. I like your hair. There's this, uh, little muscle in your neck that's kind of nice because sometimes you move your head and it defines itself. I like your voice; it comes out with a lot of vitality in it.

PHILIP: I had a feeling that if I had a sister, she'd be very much like you, because I think we're very much alike.

Philip

BOB: You're someone who looks at people's physical appearances a lot. Yet, at the same time that *you* give a very good physical impression, you're hiding your hands, you're not relaxed.

YAEL: Oh boy, when I walked in I saw you out there and I said, "Oh boy, that's what I want to see—a Hippie or a Yippie, or whatever!" (*General laughter.*) I liked especially that you had a very sen . . . have a very sensual mouth. Then I also wanted to figure out whom of the other girls did you like best. I haven't figured it out yet. (*More laughter.*)

ROBERT LEA: You're . . . uh . . . uh . . . pretty wild. I dig you. Uh, I sense that you would make a groovy friend . . . so mild, and almost as though you would not hurt anybody. Just a lovely human being, very conscious of the physical form.

BERNARD: My first impression is, uh, that you're, uh, the most . . . um . . . um . . . attractive person here. You come on with this tremendous gentle quality. I have a feeling you're not very strong, and, just to please Marty, I'd like to Indian wrestle with you because I have a feeling you're very weak.

Bernard, built like a professional wrestler, takes on Philip, who is made like a Picasso harlequin. Bernard wins quickly.

BERNARD: I'm concerned about, uh . . . whether or not you're a fag. This very gentle quality is probably confusing me. Uh, my feeling now is that you're probably not, not that it makes any difference to me. . . .

M: Can you hug him?

BERNARD: Yes, I think I can. (*He hugs Philip.*)

M: How does he feel?

BERNARD: Uh . . . I haven't hugged very many men. Uh . . . "compared to what," you know. (*General laughter.*)

M: Compared to what your conception is of hugging a man or a fag or whatever you think he is.

BERNARD: Um . . . it feels pretty good. It doesn't put me off the way I feared hugging a man would. It's not a bad feeling.

KARI: Wow, I don't like you! What I feel is that you are a New Generation, maybe just as much as Little Prince. You talk physically, yet I feel that your body is not all up to how you talk and how you emote. I feel it's, um . . . uh . . . all tangled up, all tied up in knots. There's a certain . . . agony. The "gentleness" is *not* there. You try to create an image, somehow. And that just sends me the wrong way. (*Her voice is very soft, thoughtful, subtly accented, giving a conflicting impression of profundity and total confusion.*)

> *Shershonsky speaks at length about Philip's stress on physical appearance; he assumes that Philip works in one of the art fields. A slightly negative feeling about Philip's sinuous estheticness, Shershonsky says, is mitigated by the fact that there is dirt under his fingernails. Sarah finds Philip appealing but says she has no sense of who is behind the "costume."*
>
> *Little Prince asks Philip to sit on the floor with her and then launches into a long and very romantic paean to his beauty, complete with a quotation from Malcolm Boyd on the seriousness of Young Revolutionaries.*

JANE: You seem kind of stiff and unsure. I have a sort of feeling—I don't know where it comes from—that you're very selfish.

Bernard

YAEL: When you have a body like this, why do you wear such tight pants? Why?

M: You mean when he has a body so fat?

YAEL: I didn't say fat. I feel him as maybe a little bunchier, uh, a little bulkier, than Philip, but I think, "Why does he wear such tight pants?" I feel also a lot of sadness in you.

ROBERT LEA: You have very good motivation, like the way you got up and said things to everybody. One thing that bugged me, though, was when M said would you like to hug Philip, and you like put that off. I dig grabbing guys. As a matter of fact, with friends of mine, I even ball them on the lips. It's a groovy kind of experience. But you seem very put out by that. Um, you have to assert some sort of masculinity. You want other people to recognize it, as though you're very, very unsure of yourself. (*He hugs Bernard hard, but briefly.*) You sort of tensed up your body as if it was sort of unnatural. You don't dig it.

> *Sarah feels that Bernard is up-tight; she also confesses that she is afraid of him. But after holding his hand and Indian wrestling with him, losing quickly, she decides that he is less frightening than before. Shershonsky describes Bernard as a warm, sensitive person with a cold veneer. He adds that Bernard wasn't fair in the wrestling match with Philip; that he is tense and up-tight and that he makes enemies easily.*

BOB: Rich, arrogant, very rigid in the way you think, the way you have certain categories in your mind about everything, and certainly about people. Tremendous emphasis on your own masculinity, on asserting it, as if there's some reason why you're unsure of it. . . .

> *Little Prince uses her intense and romantic approach with Bernard. She races into his arms and expresses a desire to hit, kiss, punch, and hug him. She feels that with "just a little bit of loving" he would be a complete and beautiful person.*

JANE: I think you're very hostile and kind of angry, and on the other hand I think you're very honest. I don't think you're terribly in touch with your own feelings, but I think you're honest about telling other people what you think of *them*.

PHILIP: Of all the men in the room I like you best. It's funny that you wanted to Indian wrestle with me, because what I wanted to do with you is shake your hand. But Bob is right: I think you are too concerned with physical aspects of looks instead of masculine-feminine identities. And . . . uh . . . I'd like to have a rematch with you, with Sarah refereeing it. I really didn't get a chance to put my foot down. (*To M:*) It seems to me that he is stronger than me.

M gives instructions, and the rematch begins. Philip employs a gracefulness and lightness of foot against Bernard's heavy toiling. Bernard falls off balance first, but Philip, in pulling him over, moves his own foot, thus making his victory unjudgeable.

Yael and M

Jane suggests that M do First Impressions of the participants.

YAEL: That's a good idea!

M (*to Yael*): We could share one. I think you're the one who wants to do this most.

YAEL: Oh, I'm getting scared! (*She laughs nervously as the others join in.*)

M: She really means, "M, I have some first impressions of you, and I want your first impressions of *me*."

YAEL: I wasn't so concerned about your impression of them. But their impressions of you.

M: What's yours?

YAEL: Of you?

M: No, of the man in the moon!

YAEL: The first one? (*General laughter.*) No . . . I'm gaining time. I think you're very handsome. For me, men go into two categories. The first is that I would go to bed with. And the other, I would not go to bed with. There's also a time period attached to it. Uh . . . the ones I would not go to bed with, it would even be if we had seven years on an island. You are not in that one. (*Much laughter.*) I think when I first met you the first time at a party, I wished you would be shorter. You were a little overpowering for me. But when you talked, I got a better feeling. When I first met you in that social situation, I thought, "What makes you tick?" I know that your wife liked me very much. But I felt jealous because she is tall and beautiful. And I said to myself, "Ah, why couldn't I have been very tall and beautiful?" (*She laughs, and her voice trails off.*)

M: My first impression of you was as a very lively, vivacious, bouncy kind of person, and I thought, "My God, all that energy in a four-foot package!" Very spirited. Someone I'd like to know better. You're kind of cute for a little woman of forty-odd years.

YAEL: See? I'm looking at Sarah right away! (*Much general laughter.*)

M: I'm very flattered that you found me attractive. Now, does everyone want to talk about their reactions to this stuff?

SCENE 2: REACTIONS

BERNARD: I'm very impressed how you all had the same reaction as most people who've known me for twenty-five years. It's really quite a startling phenomenon.

SARAH: It was very hard to get a first reaction without really interacting with people.

YAEL: When I walked in and said hi some people were standing around and writing things and nobody answered. You were probably told not to talk. Anyhow, I worried about it. But as time progressed, I felt very good about it. I thought, "It's very interesting how-how-how you walk into a room and people perceive you!"

SARAH: At first I found it superficial, but then I found it a great relief not to have to go through the usual things to get to know strangers.

YAEL: I wasn't told that nobody's supposed to talk! I walk in and say nicely "Hi" and nobody answers me . . . and then gives me a piece of paper and a dollar! (*The group laughs heartily.*)

SARAH: I want to say I was very relieved when the contest between Philip and Bernard turned out the way it did, because I had the feeling that Bernard could smash Philip right away, and I think that's why I was scared of him.

BERNARD (*to Philip*): I . . . I was very surprised by how strong you were. In fact, I liked the last match better than anything else I've had. I'd like to do it again, maybe later today, because you were really trying so hard. What disturbs me is that I feel I'm overly competitive, especially in athletics. I just enjoy winning for some reason. And very rarely do I find someone else who seems so anxious to win also.

PHILIP: I don't compete in athletics at all, and I'm not good for another match.

M: You said that before you drew him, too. When it wound up in a standstill.

PHILIP: Well, there was some technique involved there.

YAEL: Do any other girls like wrestling besides Sarah? I-I-I would be horrified at having to wrestle. And I am surprised . . . because she looks . . . looks like a woman, like someone who, who . . . (*To Sarah:*) Would you like to win with Shershonsky?

SARAH: No, but I like the feeling that there was some struggle involved, that there was something going on between us.

JANE: Yeah, I wanted to wrestle with Shershonsky too, just to see something happen. . . .

YAEL: Well, I would feel like tickling somebody. It wouldn't occur to me to want to wrestle!

SHERSHONSKY: Uh . . . uh, uh . . . um . . . in the second match I was rooting for Bernard because . . .

BERNARD: Because you felt sorry for what you said before?

SHERSHONSKY: No, no. I don't feel sorry for what I said before, but I had a feeling that maybe Philip was going to win. I don't know. I have this thing about rooting for the underdog to win. Usually when I'm watching a fight I get emotionally involved. But it didn't get to me, which kind of surprises me. I feel at ease here among these people, although I feel a little tense at the same time. But the perceptions of some of the people, about me, really surprised me.

M: Which people? Be specific.

SHERSHONSKY: Well, uh, Robert Lea said something about me being easygoing, and not being committed to a violent thing, but that maybe I could be hurtful. Beyond a certain point, I can cop out and get into a violent kind of thing, and on a few occasions in my life this has happened.

LITTLE PRINCE: It was really unbelievable for me! I've done a lot of work on myself up to this point, and to have people come up to me, after so little time, and tell me more than they *knew!* Robert Lea, you shocked the living daylights out of me. Because you said it was a "cerebral orgasm." And I thought, "That's the whole thing! It's Come with a Big C! Sexual intercourse with Life!" And I just don't mean physical. And when people talked about femininity and . . . about my body, I thought they were so very close, that they were picking up the child in me. And what Jane said. Fifty percent of the time, to a lot of people who don't know me, I

come across as a fake. But you said that after you got to see
me for a while, I wasn't. I liked hearing you say that.

M: One of the reasons for starting off that way is to loosen
people up. And if you're really going to get into yourself
and find out about yourself, you have to approach it through
something more than just talking. If you see children learning, they don't just look at things. They play with them,
handle them, sniff them. They take them apart and put them
together. And as grown-ups, we lose that sense—for all sorts
of reasons. I think, as Bernard said, that one of the reasons
people lose that sense is that you feel that if you touch
people, you're a sex maniac, or a pervert, or you're going to
belt somebody. There's a great holding back that cuts off a
source of pleasure that you can get turned on to again. If, in
the course of the day, you get some feelings of things you'd
like to do, you might just do them rather than talking about
them, and see what happens.

Act 2: The Most
Distressing Thing

M: I'd like everybody to think for a minute or so about what they feel is the most distressing aspect of their lives, the lives that they're living today. You'll each have three minutes.

Bernard

M hands a watch to Shershonsky and asks him to time Bernard, who begins to speak slowly, thoughtfully, seeming to reach out to the others for the first time.

BERNARD: Well, the thing that distresses me most is that people don't like me. And just as I've given this impression to everybody here in a very casual, brief encounter, I think most of the people in my life tend to react to me in the hope that I'll lose, just as Shershonsky did. Very few of my friends like me. And I think that what distresses me most is that it bugs me so much that they don't like me. I've always admired people who can just sort of come on as what they are and not give a damn whether people like them or not. . . .

Shershonsky

The watch is given to Yael.

SHERSHONSKY: Well, I . . . I think one of the things that distresses me most is that I spend an awful lot of time sort of on the outside, looking in. Being kind of hard, superficially. It's easier for me to be angry at something, easier for me to fight something, than to love something.

M: Could you be more specific?

SHERSHONSKY: Well, uh, in situations it's been very difficult for me to tell someone I really love them. I could relate to someone physically; I could really be turned on to someone. But to say, somehow, "I love you" is some kind of a locked door. I . . . I really can't . . .

M: Who in your life is it hardest to say that to?

SHERSHONSKY: To most women I've known. It's difficult for me to even say that to my wife. It's easy for me to say that to my daughter, but it's kind of hard for me to love people, to open up. I've frozen myself for a long time now. I'm sort of trying to hang loose, you know, to love people more.

ROBERT LEA: In a sense, you're afraid to expose yourself.

SHERSHONSKY: Yes, yes. That's a lot what it is.

Yael

YAEL: When I walk into a situation, I feel that everybody should love me. Uh, it's a very hard thing to have to say to myself, "All right, so some people don't dig you." The other thing is that I always appear happy, even if I'm crying inside. And from my history, I . . . uh . . . I can put on a face as if I'm the happiest person in this whole world, even while being very sad. What distresses me most, uh . . . one is that I'm getting older, and I'm stuck someplace. The other thing is that I feel if I could start over again I would do certain things differently.

M: Like?

YAEL: Studying-wise. And . . . uh . . . the other distressing thing is that I'm m-married to a very, very nice guy. Uh . . . it's not my first marriage. And I have no very great intentions about doing anything about it, but it just happens that right now it's at a stage where, uh . . . um . . . some other things should be happening.

M: It's distressing that you're married to a nice guy?

YAEL: If I were married to a guy who wouldn't be nice, I would separate. I would take my two kids whom I like very much. But I can't do that. (*There is a tightness in Yael's throat, yet she speaks quickly, almost chirpily, to hide it.*)

M: Because he's so nice?

YAEL: Because he's so nice. And I . . . I really . . . don't have any reason.

PHILIP: Do you love him?

YAEL: I don't know what love is. I don't think I've ever really loved anybody. I have lots of friends. Uh, I would not be alone, not one evening, if I don't want to. People like me, and I can lighten up groups of people. I, I like my job, but I have a feeling that whatever I'm doing now is a little late. I should be doing that ten years ago. I feel that time is running out for me.

Sarah

SARAH: One of the things that distresses me most is loneliness, which I haven't been able to cope with too well. And the other is a feeling of cowardice in not being able to express anger at someone, when I'm feeling hostile or critical. Sometimes when I'm involved with one person I can express my feelings fairly easily. But to persons in a group I find it difficult to speak up when what I have to say is negative. Part of this is, I think, a need to be liked, and the other thing is that somewhere I'm so angry and hostile that I have a real fear that I'm going to damage somebody else if I come out with what I think.

M: Do you want to get in a couple now?

SARAH: Well, I have a feeling, for instance, with Little Prince, that she was being kind of precious, and, uh . . .

M: Look her in the eye, and say "you."

SARAH: . . . and very oversentimental at times, and I really didn't trust it at all, and I felt myself getting embarrassed. There was a very saccharine quality about what you were saying. I think I find it easier to be straightforward with the guys. Particularly I find it hardest with the younger women. Mostly Little Prince, and Philip.

Little Prince

Little Prince speaks well past her allotted three minutes about the problems of being a "Love Slob," of her own indulgence in sentimentality, lyricism, grandiosity, and poetry. Then she confesses to a fear of other women on the street, based on a Simone de Beauvoir concept that when a man one loves looks at another woman, a great deal may be lost. Both Bernard and Yael find this confession incredible. Little Prince then talks about her strict Catholic education and of the fact that once she was seventeen pounds heavier. Now, however, she states, she has learned to love herself more. It is always possible that some Great Therapist from the Sky will come down and tell her that her reality is not The Reality. "But dammit," she adds, "it is!"

Philip

Philip says that, like Sarah, he is incapable of showing anger. He speaks of an older brother who used to beat him up badly whenever he took a stand and says that he is now distressed by frightening dreams in which he is mugged by strange people from whom he tries to run but can't. Little Prince and Sarah try to make him see that this is not likely to occur in reality. When Robert Lea asks him if he has ever had homosexual fantasies, he answers yes.

Jane

Jane is distressed by the fact that she is unable to initiate things on her own. She is a spectator rather than a life-participant. She would like to write but can only serve as a critic for the works of others. Robert Lea points out that she doesn't really dig herself; and she admits that while she knows why she should, she doesn't.

Kari

As Kari begins, it is almost impossible to hear her or to follow her train of thought from the tapes. She strings out her words in a vague, uncertain chain, never talking about things in the personal sense, never saying "I" or "me." The essence of her articulations is that her marriage has recently gone sour and that she is separated from her husband. Robert Lea tries to pin her down.

ROBERT LEA: Well, what is love? What is this thing, this quality?

KARI: Well, I don't know.

ROBERT LEA: Then you'll never really know whether your marriage was a worthwhile one.

LITTLE PRINCE: Do you believe in inevitable, absolute-type situations where you don't have a choice?

KARI: I do sometimes. Like somewhere we try to go beyond ourselves and then we come into biases and neuroses and all these fucking terms I hate, and you box yourself in with your thoughts, and that kind of whole dilemma is terrible. And I just feel like . . . I feel like busting it.

SARAH: You know, I find it a little hard to follow what you're saying, but are you saying that in some way you'd like to make some sense of your own life even though some things might happen—like your marriage might fall apart? Things that you hadn't figured?

KARI: It seems to me that two things should always be there: to

control or not to control. And then to have the choice of
either one. But I don't have the choice. And that's to me
horrifying.

BERNARD: Can I say something just as a point of order? I think
we're better off if everybody says what they really feel, and
tries to stay away from so many abstractions.

M: Who're you talking to?

BERNARD: I'm talking to everybody, but it's been my feeling
that several people, Kari and Little Prince, have been saying
what would look best, what people would like to hear.

KARI: Shush!

BERNARD: You're very hostile.

KARI: That's right. I get a feeling right now that I'm very angry.

BERNARD: That's what I want to hear.

KARI: Yeah. Well, I want to listen.

BERNARD: That's the first straightforward thing I've heard out
of you. That's good. If we get too abstract, nothing will be
accomplished.

KARI: Weren't *you* abstract?

BERNARD: Well, I think I was pretty straightforward. I told you
in very simple terms that I think people don't like me, and
that even my friends don't like me. One reason I came here
to spend sixteen hours—you know, time is money to me—is
because I'm interested in how people will react to me who
have no preconceptions about me. Maybe I'll find out how
terrible I am. And I think that if the others of you insist on
using abstract, philosophical phrases, you're simply skirting
around what's really bugging you.

SARAH: I agree with you completely, but it's hard to do. You've
been doing it better than some other people can.

KARI: And you're being overcritical. You're trying to take over
the situation and write it.

JANE (*to Kari*): I think he's right, and particularly in reference to you. You keep using the word "you"—a kind of third-person impersonal.

LITTLE PRINCE: Can I take thirty seconds since you've mentioned me? Whenever I use the words "neurosis," "absolute," "inevitable"—they're not abstract terms. They're the nitty-gritty of everything that's happening to me, and to a lot of people I see. Now, if you can't associate to the word "neurosis," then I shouldn't have to change my words to suit you.

M: Anytime you think somebody isn't saying it the way they should be saying it, play alter ego for them. Get behind them and say, for them, *being* them, "I really feel fucked up for this, that, and the other thing." See if you can make it concise for them, and then they'll tell you whether you're right or wrong.

SOMEONE: How about you, M?

M

M: The most distressing thing in my life is that the tape recorders may not be working properly, and everybody's been assembled here for this book.

SEVERAL PEOPLE (*simultaneously*): Come on, that's not real enough! That's not concrete enough! That's superficial! That's not really the most distressing thing!

M: That's the most distressing thing in my life. It really is.

BERNARD: You're full of shit, Marty. Let's get one thing straight: Are you going to participate in this thing, or are you going to be Olympian and occasionally come down and make wisecracks?

M: But it really is the most distressing thing in my life right now.

YAEL: Of the moment. So next time when you do a group like this, you have three machines and try them out. And I agree with Bernard. I think you should be in, and not an observer. I think it would be helpful to all of us.

M: Anytime you want to ask me something, I'll answer it.

YAEL: Oh, you're just putting yourself out, like he says, with the Olympus!

M: Well, I told you what the most distressing thing is. Believe it or not.

BERNARD: The most distressing thing in my life right now is that I have a bit of gas, that I don't want, before all these people . . . But I couldn't be serious now, Marty, if I—

M: The most distressing thing in my life is that I'm having so much technical trouble getting this down.

YAEL: It depends on the level that one wants to talk about.

M: Other things in my life are groovy. I'm doing what I want to do. It's Robert Lea's turn.

Robert Lea

Robert Lea begins by describing himself as a very happy, swinging human being, a man who loves to get up in the morning. But something does distress him: that "people are really just a bunch of fucking frauds."

SARAH: Us, or you mean other people?

ROBERT LEA: Here we happen to be honest with one another. Probably this will be a very satisfying experience. But outside, it's very difficult. Just yesterday I was with this, um . . . young, beautiful girl. Uh . . . we were drinking all afternoon, to my chagrin. I'm not really a drinker. And then we went over to her house and she knew . . . she knew she was turning me on. But when we got down to the nitty-gritty . . . well, you see, I know I could have conned this girl yesterday, but I didn't really want to, because that was not real. The real thing was we both should have really, uh, made it at that moment. But like she was tangential, and we really—

SHERSHONSKY (*shouting*): But beyond that, what distresses you?

ROBERT LEA: The dishonesty of human beings in a social situation.

LITTLE PRINCE: If a person is a fraud, that's what they are. Why don't you accept that? You want everybody to be on the same open, honest level? It's a beautiful idea, man, but it's gonna take years!

SARAH: What arouses my suspicion is that "everyone's a fraud except me."

ROBERT LEA: No, no. I can really communicate with people, but then there are certain instances where I can't, and that really turns me off.

KARI: Can I—

ROBERT LEA: Yes, doll.

KARI: You . . . you make me laugh, but yet I don't sense any sense of humor from you. What makes *you* really laugh, you know?

ROBERT LEA: Oh, I really do laugh when I get high. I really dig when my whole body swings from a laugh.

LITTLE PRINCE: But when you're not high?

ROBERT LEA: No, as a matter of fact. When I first got married I didn't turn on for three or four years, and when I started to turn on again about six years ago, just with pot, everybody said, "Gee"—like they were very glad, because I really become a very happy individual. Really, I like to laugh, though I don't look it.

KARI: No. You don't, at all. To me you look like you never would look at a joke.

SARAH: You do look solemn.

LITTLE PRINCE: I think you miss it when you're not high.

JANE: Does anything scare you?

ROBERT LEA: No. Outside of health, nothing scares me . . . that my family and I should be healthy.

SHERSHONSKY: Do you think there's some kind of a fraudulent feeling in these gales of laughter when you're high on pot? Like people might see you, and if you weren't using pot for three years, you were like down?

ROBERT LEA: Like right now I feel down. Like I'm not really, uh, ecstatic or outside of myself. And I really would like to laugh. It's one of my things. Once I was helping a writer of comical material for Phil Foster and others—and if I laughed, they used it. But I don't tell jokes, see. I'm not like a stand-up comedian.

M: You don't feel as groovy when you're off grass as when you're on?

ROBERT LEA: Right, right.

M: Are you distressed about that?

ROBERT LEA: Yeah. I like to be high all the time.

BERNARD: As I understand it, what distresses you most is the way other people behave. I find this almost unbelievable. I'm never really distressed about other people. I'm distressed about myself.

ROBERT LEA: I dig me, I like me. I like me a lot.

BERNARD: You do?

ROBERT LEA: I really do. Yeah.

KARI: I don't really think you do.

Bob

Bob, with many hesitations and apparent discomfort, states that he is distressed because he cannot form the warm relationships which Robert Lea has mentioned. He has never been able to maintain close friends. He cannot operate on a basis of equality: Either he subordinates people or overelevates them. This causes him to retire from relationships altogether.

Little Prince

This is Little Prince's second chance to express her Most Distressing Thing. She repeats that fourteen years of Catholic education has left her "with a lot of shit" and

*tries to describe a problem having to do with "exclu-
siveness as far as physicality is concerned."*

JANE: I think she's trying to say that she can only fuck one man
at a time.

LITTLE PRINCE: Right. I have that feeling of, quote, "dirty"—
and, you know, I love one man, and yet I love lots of people.

BERNARD: Why don't you say "lots of men"? You couldn't quite
say that, could you?

LITTLE PRINCE: Maybe I should have said "lots of men." I do
love men, and I'd like to love them physically, and—

M (*playing her alter ego*): "I'd like to ball lots of men."

LITTLE PRINCE: NO!!!

M (*continuing as her alter ego*): "Catholic education makes me
have to put it in terms of physicality."

ROBERT LEA: The Catholic Church really made it, they really
did their thing.

LITTLE PRINCE: Yeah.

YAEL: But what is wrong with loving one man?

LITTLE PRINCE: I feel I have to, *have to, want to* screw somebody
else, but I really don't want to, so I can stay exclusive, and
it's—

YAEL: Let's say, specifically: You could sleep with one man, and
then you would be on vacation, and you would meet another
man. You would like to be able to sleep with that other man?

LITTLE PRINCE: I can't get myself to sleep with anyone else
without feeling dirty.

BERNARD: But you want to. Let's really get down to it now.

SARAH: I don't see what's so terrible about just going to bed
with one guy.

*Little Prince goes on at length to explain that her lover
has only been to bed with two women in his life and
that he needs other women now to develop his experience, to satisfy his curiosity. She feels it would be health-*

*ier to make further explorations along with him, but
she isn't sure.*

JANE: I'm in exactly the same position you're in, except that I
don't know about the thing about getting healthy. You only
want to fuck him, and he wants to fuck a whole lot of other
chicks. Does it make him feel bad that you only want to fuck
him?

LITTLE PRINCE: No, no, it doesn't make him feel bad. I start
destroying the situation. . . . I don't want to take up that
much time. . . .

M: Okay, we won't let you.

LITTLE PRINCE: Okay.

Act 3: The Most Shameful Thing

SCENE 1: SEXUAL SHAMES

M: I'd like you to think of something else now: the thing you're most ashamed of.

LITTLE PRINCE (*moaning*): Oh, God . . .

KARI: Oh, shit.

The atmosphere is one of silent tenseness. People look into their laps or off into space. Little Prince seems the most agitated.

BERNARD (*finally*): In what area?

M: Your own area.

SARAH (*laughing*): I'll be darned if I can think of anything!

BERNARD: How does shame differ from the thing that most distresses you?

M: Well, Yael isn't necessarily ashamed over the fact that if she had a lousier husband, she'd split—but can't because he's so nice.

YAEL: It's something we actually did, then?

M: Did, felt. Some secret you've kept because it's so awful.

YAEL: I feel it's very, very simple. I have a very nice guy, and sometimes I'm very, very bitchy, or pick quarrels. Then I feel ashamed. But it's not an all-consuming shame, of making me walk around the streets saying what a horrible person I am.

M: What does he do, for instance, that makes you feel ashamed if you're not nice to him?

YAEL: He's a wonderful father, he loves me very much. He says "love"—whatever that is. I think I'm kind of ashamed that I, um . . . that I want more out of life than just being that nice picture of a woman that's supposed to be . . . I . . . I pick fights, and I know that I do it. To provoke response. And he doesn't deserve it. He's so kind yet. For sixteen hours I'm going away. He certainly didn't like it. I'm ashamed of hurting him emotionally.

M: Did he cry?

YAEL: No.

M: Did he look sad?

YAEL: No. He just said, "Have fun. Have fun at your crazy meeting there"—or something like that.

M: Did he say, "I'll miss you. How can you go away from me now"?

YAEL: No. No, no—that he wouldn't say because I would laugh at him.

M: What did he really feel?

YAEL: I think he feels threatened.

> *There is a growing tension within Yael, yet she persists in talking quickly, almost airily, in an effort to hide the real emotion.*
>
> *At this point Little Prince gets up, sits down on the hall floor near Marjorie, and has a cigarette. She is visibly agitated.*

M (*to Yael*): Tell me as if you are him. You are him.

YAEL: That I'm crazy. Here I have a nice husband and two wonderful children—

M: No, no, Yael. Talk *as* him.

YAEL: All right. "I feel that Yael is crazy. Why can't she be satisfied like all the other women, with all the things that she has that she never had before, and doesn't appreciate?"

M (*speaking to Yael as if she were the husband*): How does she make you feel?

YAEL: "Um, on the one hand, very good—when she goes to work, because she makes me feel secure, because financially it helps. On the other hand, I would really be the European type of husband who's the auth . . . authoritarian guy, and things would work . . ."

ROBERT LEA: Do you make him feel inadequate?

M: Let's keep her playing the husband. Does she make you feel inadequate?

YAEL: "Yes."

ROBERT LEA: How does she threaten you?

YAEL: "By sometimes saying that she's trapped, but . . . but not very seriously wanting to get out of it."

ROBERT LEA: She does this intentionally, doesn't she?

YAEL: "Yes, but not because she's bad. Uh, that's her way. Uh . . . I also feel intellectually threatened because I would rather have some more peace and quiet and watch television, and not be pushed, and not be dragged to all those crazy guys with long hair . . ."

ROBERT LEA: How do you let her down?

YAEL: "I haven't let her down. I would always like her. I have always b-been the same. But when I see that she goes to . . . to a group with crazy guys like M, and spends hours just sitting there, talking . . ."

M: Is she smarter than you?

YAEL: "Mmmm, I guess so. And I don't like it that she goes for a degree either, because I don't know what's happening afterwards, when I have to call her 'Doctor.' "

ROBERT LEA: Are you sexually inadequate with her?

YAEL: "Uuhhmm, I do satisfy her. But it bothers me that she doesn't want to have sex as much as I would like. Uh . . . she picks fights in order to prevent it." All right, that's enough! I've said enough!

M (*persisting*): She doesn't, then, really turn on to you? You think she's grown tired or bored with you?

YAEL (*complying again*): "Uh, yeah."

M: Well, what are you doing about it at the moment?

YAEL: "Withdrawing. . . . I can't really do anything about it because I'm not clear that all these things are happening. . . ."

M: You can always go off and see another woman, find someone who likes you who's a little dumber, who has fewer aspirations.

YAEL: "It would never occur in my mind."

ROBERT LEA: Does your wife understand you better than you understand her?

YAEL: "I guess so." Hey . . . next person!

M: No, let's stay with this. Why are you uncomfortable?

YAEL (*as herself*): Well, first of all I'm uncomfortable b-because several times it flashed through my mind that I'm really crazy. Here I have everything that someone with my background would have wanted. I . . . I actually feel that for a refugee child like myself . . . to have what I have arrives at the highest to what I could have arrived.

JANE: If it's the height, then how come you want more?

YAEL: I do not know that.

JANE: Well, then it's not the height. If there's something you want that you don't have, you should have it. Why do you feel you should be satisfied?

YAEL: I feel that someone with my background, and my height, and my looks, and with everything else, I've—

M (*playing Yael's alter ego*): "Considering that I'm tiny, that I'm ugly, and that I'm growing old, I should be satisfied with a dull husband who'd rather sit around and watch television. But I have nice children, so—"

LITTLE PRINCE (*who has returned to the group, seemingly calmed*): What happens when you do some of these crazy

things? Are you going to destroy what you have now, or can
it somehow coexist with it?

YAEL: I do not know. Sometimes I honestly do feel that I have
to do what I did once before. . . . Just to say, "That's it!"—
and take my little girl of a former marriage, and start something else. On the other hand, I say, "I cannot do that to the
children."

ROBERT LEA: You feel you're sacrificing for them, don't you?

YAEL: Yes. I have a little bit of the Jewish Master . . . uh,
Jewish Mother probably in me. I work very hard. Um . . .

M: The Jewish mother for your husband?

YAEL: The Jewish Mother syndrome of feeling sorry, of martyr-
dom. I . . . I try not to do that. Consciously, I don't want
my son to grow up like *Portnoy's Complaint*. I feel that I
should be grateful. When I look at Sarah and she says "loneliness"—I feel even stronger. I have, uh, the most gorgeous,
beautiful children that the world can produce, and I have a
husband with a secure income, and I have a home, and I
have an apartment, and . . . and everything.

JANE: You didn't do anything to get all that?

YAEL: Oh, I worked hard.

SARAH: To whom are you grateful?

ROBERT LEA: To God.

LITTLE PRINCE: What I'm wondering is—who is this great God
coming down and telling you you have to be grateful?

YAEL: You know there's a fear that when you're too happy,
when things go too well, something comes to strike it
down . . .

M: What do you think life would be like if you did leave?

YAEL: I don't think I can do it. First of all, there's no other
man that . . . that I would say I would leave here, and I
would go there. If it would be untenable, I would leave
without there being another man. I did that two times . . .
leaving, just leaving. I would really like to keep this, but

there are, I have . . . a-additionals, like, uh, what I would
really like now to have is uh . . . a very interesting lover. . . .

LITTLE PRINCE: Why can't you?

YAEL: I'm not saying I can't. I just haven't found . . .

ROBERT LEA: Isn't there in your marriage one of the most important things missing? Intellectual relationship?

YAEL: I'm a little tired, uh . . . going to bed with the same . . .
uh . . .

ROBERT LEA: Have him grow a beard. (*General laughter.*)

YAEL: I asked you to take yours off. I don't know how he would
look with one on!

M: Have you ever had a lover before, with this second husband of yours?

YAEL: Uh, no.

PHILIP: Is he very set in his European ways?

YAEL: Yes, which in many respects I do appreciate. From knowing American men, there are some qualities I don't think I
would be so pleased with . . .

M: Have you ever attempted to have a lover before? You've been
married how many years now?

YAEL: Seventeen. I had, uh, one encounter with a friend who
used to be a lover of mine before I was married. But I
wouldn't want him as a lover now.

> *Yael goes on to say that she has many nonsexual relation-
> ships with men, but that she wants to be "swept off her
> feet."*

M: Don't any men try to sweep you off—with your vivacity?

YAEL (*neatly, with precision*): No. They all have such hang-ups.
Their hang-ups would turn me off.

ROBERT LEA: Hhhmmph!

PHILIP: American men?

YAEL: All kinds. They fascinate me, especially one WASP . . .
but, uh, sex is another thing. I don't like to initiate it. This is
my third marriage. But it was always me who initiated it.

ROBERT LEA: Maybe you really have what you want and you're not aware of it.

JANE: But she's not happy with it. Her husband is a drag. You know, he doesn't really appreciate you.

YAEL: Yes, I think he should be a little bit more enthusiastic. And I know. . . . I-I-I often pick. It happens in the evening . . . we think of fights about money or things like this, in order not to have, uh, not to have relations. . . .

BOB: Um . . . the thing that I'm most ashamed of in my life is, um . . . almost a sort of rerun of *Portnoy's Complaint*. . . . It's pretty much ended now, but, well, from the time I was twelve or thirteen on, I masturbated with a great deal of frequency and was very, very ashamed of it . . . and worried that I was doing damage to myself. . . . Uh . . . um . . .

M suggests that all the men sit down on the floor with Bob in order to share this common experience.

BOB: You know . . . I would mess around, you know . . . when I could have been doing more constructive things. A number of times, especially as I got older, I would say, "Now it's time to stop, this is kid stuff." But yet, like I was going back to it. . . .

M: You dirty old fox. (*Laughter.*)

BOB: I was married, uh, about a month ago, but it's still something which, you know . . . which stays in my mind. . . .

SHERSHONSKY: Did you like it better than screwing?

BOB: No.

SHERSHONSKY: Well, what's to be ashamed of?

PHILIP: It's just supposed to be bad.

BOB: Right. That's it.

ROBERT LEA: It's a dirty thing to do, isn't it? Terribly dirty and filthy! It's really a *groove!* (*He laughs.*)

M: Can you loosen your belt, slip your hand into your pants, and talk to us while you're touching your cock?

Bob is taken aback, but he follow's M's instructions. His

hand is now on his penis, and his speech is wavering, con-
fused, hard to follow. The group attention paid to this
act is deliberately strong, seeming to be forced, particu-
larly among the women, who retain their seats outside
the circle of men.

BOB: Yes . . . um . . . I don't . . . uh . . . I did feel ashamed
then, in the past . . . I think, I guess . . .

ROBERT LEA: Well, experiment now and see if you feel the same.

BOB: Yeah . . . uh . . . (*He continues to touch himself.*)

M: How do you feel, sitting there that way?

BOB: Uh . . . no reaction.

M: *None?* (*There is sudden uproarious laughter from the men.*)

BOB: I feel as if there is no reaction. . . .

M: Does your hand feel your penis, or does your penis feel your
hand, or both, or neither, or what?

BOB: My hand feels the penis.

M: See if you can let the penis feel the hand.

BOB (*after a pause*): To a certain extent, it can.

M: Let's all join him. (*He puts his hand inside his pants.*)

BERNARD (*shouting quickly*): I don't feel like it myself!

M: Okay, you don't have to.

   Shershonsky tries the experiment, but the others refrain.

PHILIP (*to Bob*): You're accustomed to sleeping with your wife
every night?

BOB: Yeah.

PHILIP: What if she took a vacation? Would you be tempted to
masturbate?

BOB: Uh, I . . . I probably would be.

BERNARD: What do you think's wrong with it? Your Jewish upbringing?

BOB: Yeah, uh, probably . . . I mean . . .

M: What do you think we all think of you so far? Tell each of us.

BOB: I don't know. Nobody else put their hands in their pants,
you know, and I think—

M: Shershonksy did, briefly, and I did. What does that mean to you?

BOB: I think, uh, you may all share the same kind of things, at least to a certain extent. You know, in part we've all gone through it. . . . It's not unique. But that doesn't lessen in any real sense the . . . the feeling of shame I had, and have. . . .

M: Let's all tell him a story about masturbation. The person who speaks, sit in front of him and tell it.

ROBERT LEA: Uh, I felt the same way you do until I realized what goes on in my head goes on in everyone's head. Yesterday, after I couldn't consummate a relationship with this beautiful, young thing, I went home and masturbated. And I do whenever the spirit grabs me. Every day, every other day. I like doing it!

BERNARD: Do you prefer that to intercourse?

ROBERT LEA: Well, I . . . I equate it with it. I'm not partial to it.

M: I was playing around when I was a kid around eleven or twelve, and all of a sudden this thing got hard, and then, suddenly, fluid shot out. I ran downstairs, was sure my parents knew what I was doing, and I felt very uncomfortable. Then I went through years of locking the bathroom door. I also felt it was a pretty funny, special, creepy thing to do because no one talked about it. I still can enjoy masturbation—probably because I've been a sperm donor since I was in medical school, and every now and then a gynecologist calls up and says, "Hey, send us down some right now!" (*Laughter from the women.*) So I pick out all the juicy females I know—patients, my wife, my friends' wives, other people—and have them to my heart's content. Another story that comes to mind —why I don't know—occurred about two summers ago. I was out sailing alone in the middle of Peconic Bay, and the sun was coming down, you know, and I had on a bathing suit, and the sun was just pouring on me, and suddenly I had the feeling, "My God, what a gassy thing it would be to drop my pants and masturbate on the spot." And I did. It was kind of a wild experience. But I can't put into words what it was about. The sun, the sailing, being out there in the middle of the bay, with people off in the distance not knowing what the pretty sailboat was doing, but it was nice.

PHILIP: Actually, I have never masturbated. I've played with myself fairly frequently, but coming to orgasm by self-manipulation . . . I won't do it, no matter how horny I get.

ROBERT LEA: What is there you don't like about it?

PHILIP: It's the nature of . . . of what it is in society. . . .

SHERSHONSKY: You won't even, uh, touch your cock now?

PHILIP: Well, I'd probably be embarrassed. . . .

M: Try it anyway.

PHILIP: I know it's there.

M: We know you have it.

> *Philip complies. He says that it feels all right, that he is not ashamed of it, but that he would never manipulate to orgasm. Bernard states that he supports Philip in this view and could not consider masturbation when there is an availability of women. It strikes him as "abnormal."*

ROBERT LEA: Do you feel it's "dirty"?

BERNARD: I didn't say that. I just simply do not find myself stimulated by it.

M: I'm struck by the similarity between the approach to your cock, and your approach to people. There's an aversion to using your hands.

BERNARD: Yeah, uh . . . and yet I consider myself more lecherous than maybe ninety percent of the men in this world.

M: All the more surprising. It's almost as though touching sets up an inhibition process.

BERNARD: A touch, by me, cannot do it. It can't be another man, and it can't be myself.

ROBERT LEA: If you can't dig this part of yourself, how can you expect someone else to?

BERNARD: I don't think that necessarily follows. (*He is becoming slightly, but perceptibly, annoyed and turns to the group for affirmation of his sexual stand.*)

M: Shershonsky, sit in front of Bernard and tell him a story about masturbation.

SHERSHONSKY: Yeah. Well, uh, I have masturbated, and do, and will. For a while I felt a little guilty about it, but then I did some reading and talking to people, and it, uh, never, uh, was really a hang-up. . . .

> *He then tells a story about a beautiful young girl who stood on a balcony when he and his Army buddies were marching by. She seemed to be flaunting her sexuality at them, and later he masturbated successfully, using her in his fantasy. He says he finds it harder to talk about it than to do it; and adds that he would not want his children to feel defensive about it.*

M: Bob, How do you feel about yourself now?

BOB: Well, it's good to know that people don't only pass through it, but they—

ROBERT LEA: But they remain in it.

BOB: They remain in it. That's right! (*Bob and Robert Lea begin to laugh.*)

JANE: Can I say something from a woman's point of view?

> *Jane says that she is amazed that men are ashamed of masturbation; that every man she has ever known does it, including the man she lives with.*

YAEL: But would it bother you if he would have intercourse with other women?

JANE: Yeah, it has.

M (*to Yael*): Would it bother you if your husband did?

YAEL: It's . . . it's inconceivable. But yes, it would bother me.

LITTLE PRINCE: I'm just wondering if any of you have ever considered the idea of whether or not women masturbate.

BOB: I know they do.

M: How do you know?

BOB: From reading. (*Much general laughter.*)

M: Ask each one of them individually. Start with Yael.

YAEL: Start with somebody else for a change!

> *The laughter which ensues in this period is less tense than it was earlier. It is now less an expression of individual anxiety, and more one of camaraderie.*

SARAH: Actually, I don't remember masturbating very much.

M: Have you ever?

SARAH: Hhmmnn. Yeah, I have. But I've never been able to bring myself to climax that way. But, uh, most women do. It's sort of unnatural not to.

JANE: I masturbated all through high school, and in fact, uh, I frequently brought myself to climax. But when I started fucking, I stopped masturbating.

> *Little Prince relates how she masturbated when she was young, told her mother about it, and was considered to be a sinner, thereafter being forced to go to confession. Later she read a book by Albert Ellis and decided to beat her guilt. At present she masturbates successfully whenever her lover is away.*

KARI: I never remember masturbating when I was a child, but I remember seeing my mother now. And, uh, my children . . .

M: How about you, though?

KARI: I don't remember! I just complete, uh, a cutoff! I've tried and I cannot come to a climax masturbating! (*She is suddenly high-pitched and shouting.*)

M: How do you do it?

KARI: With the finger.

M: Where?

KARI: In my vagina. The clitorial . . . uh, you know. I, uh, become excited, and at a certain point the feelings just turn off, completely off! And when I can't remember from childhood, I know something's wrong. It smells rotten. . . .

BERNARD (*interposing quickly*): The *story* smells wrong.

M: How about the secretions. Did you ever sniff them?

KARI: Yeah. Uh, it doesn't smell bad.

BERNARD (*playing Kari's alter ego*): "Why does my story smell rotten? I'm not telling the truth."

M: Yael?

YAEL: I thought you were going to forget about me!

> *Yael tells of a boy she knew at an orphanage where she was put as a child. They played with each other sexually, which saved her from masturbation. At present, however, she does it and can come to orgasm; but she prefers to be "held by a man." She adds that she wishes she had known earlier that it is "normal."*

KARI: My father used to be a masturbator . . . plus being a religious fanatic at the same time. It was quite hard to—

BERNARD: How did you know he was a masturbator?

KARI: Well, because, uh, I would come into a room and there my father would be, and, uh, the bed would be going, and then of course he would stop abruptly, and put his hand up, and then he was left hanging in the air. And that made fights with my mother, so then, of course, it got clarified . . . the omen on masturbation, the guilt . . . When you have these guys masturbating on the roofs . . . we happen to have one across from us, and it can just . . . just drive me crazy!

M: Like Daddy?

KARI: Uh-huh, like Daddy. It just used to drive me crazy. And I mean I caught this guy at it. . . . I hate . . . all that shit . . . and I'd scream! Aaaaaauuuuggghhh! (*It is a real scream and seems to be for the moment as well as for the past.*)

M: You can just keep on feeling guilty about this forever, if you like, or—

LITTLE PRINCE: Yeah, it's such a habit—feeling guilty.

YAEL: That's very interesting, that it's a habit. Will the next generation be completely sexually free?

LITTLE PRINCE: After three more generations.

YAEL: You really think it will come?

LITTLE PRINCE: Yeah. Oh, god, yeah. It certainly will.

PHILIP: It's very near.

YAEL: I know that in the kibbutz the original idea was free sex, and it just didn't work.

LITTLE PRINCE: What I'm hoping for is that there will be enough *I Am Curious (Yellow)*'s, and enough masturbation, and enough orgies, and enough wife-swapping so that it will all get into its perspective. It won't be the Almighty Cock anymore. It'll just *be*.

JANE: Beautiful!

SHERSHONSKY: I'd just like to dump one thing, if you're all listening. When I was a kid a man took me up to his apartment to give me joke books and some candy. And, uh, he started to fondle me and show me all sorts of pictures with all kinds of sex in them. And then he made me, uh, jerk him off. And I was sort of crying, you know . . . and well, he came, and I was very sick, really shook up, and there was nobody to tell it to. Things were rather bad between me and my father then, and I couldn't tell anyone. And then this caused another funny situation. I was going to a Jewish religious school for kids, and there was this young teacher there, and he used to put his arm around me, and one day he showed me some dirty matchbook covers and he pinched me a little. And this got me very unhappy, and I set fire to the school. I made this tremendous stink bomb with a strip of film, and set fire to it outside his door, and they had to let all the kids out of school. And then they kicked me out. They called up my home and they said, you know . . . I'm a degenerate and they don't want me there anymore. . . .

M: What made it so hard for you to tell this before?

SHERSHONSKY: Well, I was kind of locked up. I had a rigid father and I just couldn't talk to him. He'd have beaten me. . . .

YAEL: What about your mother?

SHERSHONSKY: Well, the same thing. But it was very disturbing, because it was the guy that showed me the pictures and pinched me that called up my house in such great indignity, and you know . . . The Voice of School . . . "Your son . . . I have to bring this to your attention, Mrs. _____. You have a very dangerous, sick son there. He set fire, and we're gonna have to kick him out." It just seemed like such a big injustice, and I couldn't tell anyone. . . .

M (*sitting behind Shershonsky and playing his alter ego*): "I didn't talk about it because I thought maybe there was something funny about me, that I was giving off funny signals that would *make* the schoolteacher and the other guy try these things with me. I was so ashamed people would see *me* as a pervert that I kept it in."

SHERSHONSKY: Uh-huh. That could be. . . .

ROBERT LEA: You just had an orgasm, Shershonsky.

SHERSHONSKY: What?

ROBERT LEA: A mental orgasm. You just got rid of this massive load.

SHERSHONSKY: Yeah. That's out now. It's nice to have it out.

M: You don't know what to do with a thing like that as a kid.

SHERSHONSKY: No.

M: I had this thing happen in a movie house when I was about twelve. My younger cousin and my parents went to a movie, and some older guy came in and said, "Hey, I came in late. Will you tell me what the movie was about?" So I said, "Yes, I will." And he said, "Is it all right if I put my hand on your knee? I'm nervous." So I said, "Okay." But then he started to go like this. . . . (*M demonstrates the man's hand moving up M's leg.*) You know, I started to feel a little bit uncomfortable. So I put my hand in my pocket and jammed it over my testicles. And he kept going up, and twisting my hand, and I said to my cousin, "Let's walk to the back or something." We walked to the back, and I still didn't know what to do. And when we came back, I thought, "I know what I'll do. I'll put my cousin onto him." (*General laughter.*) And this guy had the effrontery to say to my cousin, "Switch seats with that kid." (*More laughter.*) And I didn't know what to do, so I switched seats back. And again the whole thing started off. Shit! That thing kept up for about an hour or so, and then (*M laughs*) he finally got discouraged and left. I *could* talk to my father, but I didn't know what I was telling him, except I said, "Hey, you know something funny was happening with this man who kept touching me, and he said he was nervous, and I tried to change seats with Michael." And my father said at this point, "Ah-hah . . . that man is a strange degenerate, and if it ever happens again, you better tell me." But it was interesting because I didn't know what to do with it. I didn't know what to do.

Shershonsky and Yael tell M he was lucky that he could tell his father.

SARAH: I can remember when I was that age and there would be a guy trying to feel me up, and I didn't really know exactly what was going on. I sort of knew, but I didn't. And I didn't want to be rude. (*Much general laughter.*)

Yael recalls having been seen sitting in a man's lap in the park, and being spanked unjustly for it by her parents. Later, in another country, an unmarried uncle made advances to her from time to time.

M: If we're talking about shame, let's get into what's most current, because—

YAEL: M, do you have a bathroom?

M (*pointing the way*): Sure.

SCENE 2: BERNARD'S HANG-UP

BERNARD: I have a very strange sexual hang-up that I've never confessed to anyone before, and I've always been curious as to what people's reactions would be to it.

M: Whose reaction would you be most curious about?

BERNARD: Partly in Sarah's, because she's the, you know, closest to the norm here.

M: Okay. Sit directly facing Sarah.

BERNARD: I'd rather not. I can tell it better spontaneously.

M: Give it a chance.

BERNARD (*facing Sarah*): When I was about seven or eight there was a girl in my class who was much taller than the boys, including myself. And what gave me a charge was the fact that she was so physically larger than myself. I didn't know about sexual relations until about fifth grade, but I had strong sexual feelings. I would occasionally play with her, get on top of her, and this fantasy never left me. Obviously, it was just the beginning, and . . . uh, um, uh . . . and if anything, it increased as I grew older. And I've always had a great sexual interest in women larger than myself. But I don't very often meet women larger than myself, so I have to fantasize it about large women with small men. I was, uh, at a summer camp a few years ago and one of the campers was a very little boy who always got hung up on the big girls. He would walk with these girls, and, uh, I got tremendously aroused by this, um, fantasy.

M: What fantasy?

BERNARD: The fantasy is of getting a male sort of phagocytized by this large woman, and being made helpless by her.

SARAH: What are your theories about it?

ROBERT LEA: It seems to me you consider yourself a big prick, and you want to get entirely into this, uh, into this womb . . .

M (*to Bernard*): Can you lie down on the floor, on your back, and close your eyes? Then go into the fantasy bit.

BERNARD (*lying down*): The typical fantasy I have is making love to an enormous black woman who sort of lifts me up, and, uh, I can't even reach her breasts from where I stand, so she has to lift me up. And then I suckle them, and then she lifts me higher and I'm able to kiss her. She is the one who is totally in control of the sexual situation. If she wanted to allow me to penetrate her, she would have to lift me up to do it. She's much too strong for me to, uh . . . to try to penetrate.

M: Keep your eyes closed. Is there anyone here like that woman?

BERNARD: I suppose Kari comes closest, but doesn't completely fulfill this.

M: It all takes place standing up?

BERNARD: No. I have a variety of, uh, variations.

> Bernard explains that in one of his variations the woman lies on top of him. M suggests that all the women lie on top of Bernard in order to simulate the weight and bulk of a three-hundred-pound Negress. Kari, Little Prince, Jane, and Sarah comply. Yael does not join them. Bernard describes the stimulation he feels and begins to have an erection. He speaks of all this in a blushing, self-conscious, and intellectualized style. The women heaped upon him are genuinely moved by his story and are eager to be of help. After acknowledging the erection, he states that it makes him uncomfortable and that he wishes to know what the others think about it.

M: Who in particular?

> Bernard, still beneath the pile of women, eyes closed, claps his hands to Little Prince's back.

LITTLE PRINCE: It's a groovy fantasy. Beautiful! Enjoy it.

BERNARD: I can understand a little guy who wants to be a big guy, but for a fairly big guy to have a fantasy about being a little guy, sexually, is really perverse. . . .

JANE: Are you ever passive in bed?

BERNARD: Never.

JANE: Would you like to be?

BERNARD: No. I'd be ashamed of being passive in bed. I'm afraid that, uh, all the men would feel that I'm not a good lover if I tried to, uh, be passive. . . .

JANE: I think you have to allow yourself to do whatever you feel like doing.

SARAH: I enjoy it a lot in bed if a guy sort of relaxes and lets me be active for a while.

JANE: Yeah. I often get turned off when a guy is so active he doesn't give me a chance.

LITTLE PRINCE: Yeah. It makes me feel like all I'm doing is being passive.

BERNARD: You like to be more active?

LITTLE PRINCE: I like to be both. I like to lay back and enjoy it and then when I'm ready, get on top of him and do it. I dig seeing him do nothing, just breathing and groaning. . . . Do women *make* you be active?

BERNARD: Yes.

LITTLE PRINCE: They won't allow you sometimes to—?

SARAH: Gee, it's nice sometimes just to feel helpless . . . but I guess it's hard for a guy to be that way.

BERNARD: Yeah. You're not allowed to.

M: You're allowed to. We just allowed you to.

JANE: Yeah.

BERNARD: Well, my own interpretation of this has been, it's, uh, an infantile drive. . . . My mother must have been this anonymous woman suckling me . . . with whom I'm totally helpless. . . .

M: That's your whole big put-down on things that are less ma-

ture, and less manly and tough and strong. Sex is a combination of infantile-exfantile . . . all sorts of "tiles."

LITTLE PRINCE: You feel what we just did is not normal?

BERNARD: Uh, it doesn't hang me up. It increases my sexuality.

M: How can you play it out at home?

KARI (*giggling*): How about masturbation for a start?

BERNARD: I can't.

M (*mockingly*): That's right. That's an infantile fantasy, isn't it?
I mean, kids do that before they have women.

ROBERT LEA: And men do it after they have women. (*Laughter.*)

M: Close your eyes and tell me the most passive thing you can
think of doing with your wife.

BERNARD: I suppose my greatest fantasy would be to be totally
paralyzed, lying in bed, getting an enormous erection. And
my partner, at her will, would insert it and bring me to orgasm. I would be totally incapacitated.

M: Have you ever asked your wife to do something like that?

BERNARD: No. I wouldn't dare.

LITTLE PRINCE: Why?

BERNARD: Oh, I would never admit this to her.

LITTLE PRINCE: But why?

BERNARD: I would be terribly ashamed.

JANE: What do you think she would do about it?

M: She'd probably like it.

LITTLE PRINCE: Yeah.

ROBERT LEA: She might be overawed.

LITTLE PRINCE: What could happen that would be so awful? She
might not think that you're a man? You'd lose your masculinity?

BERNARD: I would never want my wife to think I had any sexual
hang-ups.

LITTLE PRINCE: *What?*

BERNARD: Because it's . . . um . . . uh . . .

PHILIP: It's not a hang-up.

BERNARD: I keep calling it a hang-up, don't I. . . .

JANE: If you just said to her one night, "I want to be completely passive, and just have you fuck me."

ROBERT LEA: Tell her you're tired. (*Much laughter.*)

M now suggests that Bernard play two roles: that of himself, speaking to his wife, and that of his wife, answering. When Bernard finds this too difficult, M shows him how by playing Bernard's role, using Little Prince as the wife.

M (*to Little Prince*): "Look, when we go to bed tonight, I want to lie back perfectly helplessly, not move a muscle. That would really turn me on."

BERNARD: No, no! I don't really want to do this with my wife! My wife actually *is* a very sexually aggressive woman, but it doesn't turn me on. The reason is, I suppose, that—

M: Forget the analysis. Is there a woman in your present life you'd like to do it with?

BERNARD: Oh, yes.

M: Someone else you're making it with?

BERNARD: I'm not, but I'd like to be.

M: Is she someone you could approach in the next few days and ask her?

BERNARD: She'd probably slug me.

M: Try it with your wife, then. (*The women laugh.*) Play it out.

BERNARD: Who . . . who do you want to have play my wife?

M: Someone you're screwing. You can't do it with someone you're not screwing.

BERNARD: Well, one of my fantasies is making it with this Russian shot-putter. What's her name? Olga Something. I always follow how far she's putting the shot. And, uh . . . I identify with the shot. (*He tries to laugh.*)

M: First it was a Negress; second, it was a shot-putter. You want to be overpowered, right?

BERNARD: But I don't want to do it with my wife!

M: All right, all right—afterwards you can do it with someone else. But now I want you to pretend it's your wife. You're going to go home and tell her you want this thing, but that you were always afraid to ask her because you thought she'd think you weren't enough of a man.

BERNARD: (*to an imaginary wife*): "I think what we might try sometime is, I'll come home, and you can give me a spinal, a low spinal, and then I can act out this role of being . . . uh, of being a paraplegic."

Little Prince bursts into laughter.

BERNARD (*extremely distressed*): You see? She thinks it's really perverse!

M: Is your wife equipped to give you a low spinal?

BERNARD: Uh . . . no.

ROBERT LEA (*with several others*): What's a low spinal? What is that?

M: It's an anesthetic. It paralyzes you.

ROBERT LEA: Oh, that's wild! I would dig that!

BERNARD (*to his wife again*): "I think this would be a very, very wild thing. We could then, uh, make furious love."

M: "*You* could make furious love with *me!*" (*An explosion of laughter.*)

YAEL: Uh, isn't a certain part of your body also paralyzed when you . . . ?

BERNARD: She'd give it to me low enough so that—

M: For God's sake, will you play it straight?

BERNARD (*trying again*): "Would you be interested in . . . ?"

M: "NO!" (*Much laughter.*)

LITTLE PRINCE (*as the wife; gently*): "Tell me what you want, Bernard."

BERNARD: "I would like, tonight, for a change—something new: to have you give me a low spinal."

M (*now playing alter ego to Little Prince's wife role*): "You know I don't give low spinals!" (*Much laughter.*)

LITTLE PRINCE: "Tell me what you want, what you really want. . . ."

BERNARD: "I want you to paralyze both of my lower legs, and just, uh, lay me on my back, and, uh, manipulate me, and bring me to orgasm inside of you."

LITTLE PRINCE: "You mean you'd like me to make you come? I don't see why I have to paralyze your legs."

M (*to Bernard*): Shift seats now. Be your own wife, and talk to me. I'm Bernard.

BERNARD (*speaking as his wife*): "Well, this is really absurd! What's wrong with the way we've been doing it? This could be a very dangerous thing, and moreover—I'm not even sure I'd like it this way."

M: Now switch back. Be you, talking to your wife.

BERNARD: "Well, if you really like me and you really want to give me some pleasure, I think you could put aside your own feelings of . . . uh . . . uh . . . repugnance about this. I can assure you it's not dangerous, and, uh, nobody has to know about it. . . ."

M: Now be your wife again.

BERNARD: "Well, okay. We'll try it once. Now, how do you give a low spinal?" (*Laughter.*)

YAEL: Why does he have to say it with words? Why can't he just lean back and try it?

BERNARD (*eager to stop*): Who's next?

M: Are you going to do it?

BERNARD: I'll . . . I'll try it tonight. Yeah.

BOB: Why do you think you said first that the three-hundred-pound woman should be black?

BERNARD: It's better that way. It makes her more savage, more—

ROBERT LEA: Primitive.

BERNARD: Right. That's the word.

PHILIP: And you think all this is very uncommon?

BERNARD: Yes, I do think so.

PHILIP: Eldridge Cleaver has this theory about how the effete white man turns to the Amazon black woman . . .

BERNARD: Let me ask the men here. Has anybody else had this sort of a fantasy?

ROBERT LEA: Oh, yes.

BOB: Certainly not in that much detail. But I've had similar thoughts. . . .

BERNARD: Let me ask the women. Have you ever wanted a very small, passive mate as a sort of kick?

LITTLE PRINCE: I don't think size matters.

BERNARD: It's very important!

LITTLE PRINCE: I think you made her so overpowering because even in your fantasies you weren't allowing yourself to "do it." In some of my fantasies, I've had to be overpowered. It had to be a huge person with a knife all the time.

JANE: Yeah. You have to make it absurd. I feel the way she does. It has nothing to do with size. It's just that sometimes you want to be passive.

LITTLE PRINCE: To have someone be awful and really overpower you.

M: I dig a woman coming on strong and me just lying back. Of course, it makes hassles because your wife wants the same thing sometimes. (*Laughter.*)

YAEL: Why-why-why does Bernard have to *live* it out?

JANE: Because he considers it a hang-up.

YAEL: But let's suppose that he would be convinced from today that it's not a hang-up.

BERNARD: Well, I must say I'm really relieved to find out it's not such a way-out thing.

M: If a fantasy gives you pleasure, and it's not hurting anybody, and it's not making you crazy or growing hair on your palms, then why not enjoy it?

YAEL: Well, I agree, but why should he live it out? Why can't it stay a fantasy?

M: Often fantasy is an expression of what we would like to do, but don't have the courage to do, because we're embarrassed or ashamed. But if you want to live your life more adventuresomely, you can try doing more things. If you've been through a Freudian analysis, you're not supposed to *do* anything—just *understand* everything. So if you want to, you can just sit back there and say, "I know . . . it's related to my mother!" (*Several people laugh softly.*)

SCENE 3: SMALLER BUGGINGS

YAEL (*to M*): I'm bothered by something. I would like to have a verbal promise from you that whatever would happen here, would stay here. I didn't want to come at all. And when you asked everybody to get on top of Bernard, I thought I would be crushed. And I'm worried about your being able to keep whatever happens here . . . as much anonymity as—

M: What would happen? Someone might tell that nice husband of yours that you were in a pile with four other people?

YAEL: I'm not thinking of my husband. That's very interesting —that I was not thinking about him. I was thinking about some friends.

M: Who?

YAEL: That you and I know.

M: What would I do?

YAEL: At the next cocktail party, you'll be high, or they'll be high, and you'll talk. . . .

M: No, no. But you know, of course, we'll be using some of the material if it ever comes out of the tapes.

YAEL: Yes, yes. That doesn't bother me. It's just a sudden worry that . . . I don't know . . .

M: That I'll make fun of you outside of here?

YAEL: I just wanted to have, you know, like a pat on the back, saying, "Don't-don't-don't worry. . . ."

M (*patting her on the back*): "Don't-don't-don't worry." (*They both laugh.*)

YAEL: Even when you're high?

M: Even when I'm high. Are you still worried?

YAEL: I'll tell you in another hour.

M: Suppose you did something freaky in the next couple of hours. What would it be?

YAEL: Well . . . suppose I would, um, sleep with somebody . . . uh . . . Then you, at the next cocktail party, would relate that.

M: Who would you like to sleep with right now?

YAEL: Nobody, particularly.

ROBERT LEA: You just put us all down.

BERNARD: That's the biggest put-down of the day!

SARAH: I have something right now I'm ashamed of. (*She speaks from the doorway to the hall.*)

M: Could you come closer, nearer the mike?

SARAH: I'm smoking a cigarette. That's why I'm out here.

M: You can have it in here if you've got to have it.

> Sarah comes back in and confesses her shame about smoking when, for quite some time, she has been trying to give it up. Her reason for wanting to quit is her fear of lung cancer, but her shame is based on her lack of character. Finally the group uncovers her sudden anxiety and the compulsion to smoke as relating to her feeling in the Bernard Pile-Up that her tenderness might have been mistaken for sexual desire.
>
> A second anxiety-making factor was her feeling that maybe her breasts were too small for the role of sexual woman. Bob assures her that they are not.

When Bernard says that his overpowering-woman fantasy is also jacked up by the idea of a woman who is intellectually brighter than he is, Sarah is relieved. She has always, she tells him, felt that men would like her more if she were not so intelligent.

SCENE 4: LITTLE PRINCE'S FREAK-OUT

LITTLE PRINCE: For a long time I've been ashamed of my body.

M: What part of it?

LITTLE PRINCE: All of it. You know, I used to be fat. For a while I was so fat I couldn't touch myself here. (*She indicates lower abdomen and genital area.*) It was just rolls of fat. And I thought my breasts were small. And my thighs really killed me. And recently, m-mainly because we were living on ten dollars a week, I became a model, and I'm doing some nude. This is not an occupation. I did it because the money is very good. And I've been trying to be rational about it. But things come back from the body. Hang-ups. It's the idea of being dirty, of being ashamed. . . . Like I went up to Cambridge, and I slept with a guy. I had to shower, I was so ashamed of what I had done. I was all dirty. And maybe I was being untrue to myself. And I felt ashamed.

JANE: What's the connection between the incident at Cambridge and being ashamed of being fat?

LITTLE PRINCE: Sometimes I really dig my body, yet it's a source of great concern. It's so petty I want to transcend the whole thing, and yet I can't. Or won't.

ROBERT LEA: Do you want to be desired for your body, or your mind?

LITTLE PRINCE: Somebody said something to me. They said that if my lover Art slept with, or was attracted to another woman's body, then my qualities of creativity and childlikeness would just all fall away.

JANE: You're afraid that if he were attracted to somebody else's body, he would forget all the great things about you?

LITTLE PRINCE: Yeah. And it's like if I'm lying in bed with him . . . I . . . I was fantasizing last night, and he rolled over and said something like "I love you"—and I felt guilty that I was taking time away from him by fantasizing. . . .

She goes on to explain at some length that the basic problem beneath all these anxiety symptoms is the fact that she believes her body is "dirty."

M (*playing Little Prince's alter ego*): "In case you haven't noticed, folks, I have a body. I used to be ashamed of it, but now, you see, it's better. I have a body all right!"

PHILIP: You like to be complimented?

LITTLE PRINCE: Yeah, but it just kinda falls by the wayside. It doesn't make any difference.

M: "Does anybody notice my body?"

KARI: Can't you believe the compliments? Why not?

LITTLE PRINCE: Well, it's nice to hear, but I get up-tight about it.

M (*persisting*): "As soon as you say nice things, I get up-tight because I know I want you to say them. And I should be interested in more worldly things than just the concern about my body and wanting to hear nice things about it."

LITTLE PRINCE: Yeah, I want to transcend it, but I'm stuck.

KARI: Can you receive compliments?

LITTLE PRINCE: Yeah, sure.

KARI: You just said you couldn't.

M (*continuing to play her alter ego*): "I'm a model, too—in case you haven't noticed! I have a body!"

LITTLE PRINCE (*laughing*): But like all these people, you know, making different remarks, making sounds . . . it doesn't mean anything. Like they'll do it to anybody in a skirt.

ROBERT LEA: Wouldn't you be bugged if you didn't turn anybody on in this room?

LITTLE PRINCE: No, that doesn't upset me as much as I think it does. You can't be without a body. . . . But I myself would probably turn you off in some other way. Like I'm really worried about whatever I've been saying here today.

M: "I don't really believe I'll turn you off. I just sort of *said* that so you can tell me I turn you on."

JANE: No, what she's saying is that if it weren't for her body, she would—

M: I know what she's saying. But what is she *feeling?*

LITTLE PRINCE: I keep thinking I shouldn't be saying these things. . . .

ROBERT LEA: Yes, you should.

LITTLE PRINCE: But I've spoken a lot today, and I don't feel easy about it.

ROBERT LEA: Would you feel bad if all the men in the room walked out while you were talking?

LITTLE PRINCE: I'd get over it. It wouldn't be that bad.

ROBERT LEA: Oh, but you'd be very bothered, very upset.

SHERSHONSKY: Could you have come here in a very dumpy, sacky dress, with your hair pulled back in a very severe bun? How would you have felt?

Little Prince begins to ramble incoherently.

M (*stepping in quickly as alter ego*): "The thing I'm ashamed of, folks, is being so turned on and preoccupied with my own body. Wow, it's quite a body! But I should really be above all that shit."

ROBERT LEA: Right, right.

LITTLE PRINCE: It's not! It's not—

JANE: Do you dig your body?

LITTLE PRINCE (*beginning to crack under the onslaught*): Sometimes I do, but a lot of the time I hate it!

BERNARD: I think the trouble with you is that you sometime developed an image of yourself which was displeasing. Whether
it was related to the fact that you were fat, or that you were
dirty and worthless, I don't know. You lost the weight, but
you never lost the image of feeling undesirable and turning
people off.

LITTLE PRINCE (*wearily*): Everything has to be intense. . . .

BERNARD: You have to demonstrate your body nude. You have
to wear an outfit that calls attention to your beautiful
body. . . .

ROBERT LEA: You're not sure that what came out of the cocoon
was a butterfly or a moth.

LITTLE PRINCE: Yeah . . . but I wore this thing because, uh, I
kind of feel . . . uh, maybe all this is intellectual garbage, but—

M: I think it is. So why don't we cut it and move on?

LITTLE PRINCE: Yeah, let's cut it.

M: I'm tired of hearing about your body.

LITTLE PRINCE: Okay.

M: It's a very nice body, but I don't want to hear about it anymore. Touching it is one thing, but listening to it is another.

LITTLE PRINCE: Yeah.

M: Who wants to be next?

> *Little Prince is silent. She is off the hook: a momentary
> respite.*

ROBERT LEA: All right . . . my most shameful moment . . . there
were a few of those. One of the earliest I can remember is
when I was doing exercises with my mother. I must have been
about thirteen. She was wearing a nightgown, and, uh, her
breast fell out, and I got an erection. Then, later on, I slept
in the same room as my sister when I was twenty-four and she
was thirty-one. And I used to wait up for her to come home
at night so I could see her get undressed. I really wanted to

have a thing going on with my sister. But I never would approach her. And, uh, smelling her panties used to turn me on. . . . Right now it turns me off even to think about her. Uh, the latest thing was a couple of years ago, screwing my best friend's wife. Very pretty, and a real sexual freak. And I just saw her about a week ago, and we seem to have another thing going. What she wants is for me to bring another guy up to her house. She wants both of us to really work her over. But I don't want to do it. Because once I do it, it will destroy one of my freaky fantasies.

M: If you destroy a fantasy, there aren't many left?

ROBERT LEA: Right, right.

JANE: You mean once you've done it the idea doesn't turn you on anymore?

ROBERT LEA: Right. Once you act out a fantasy—

M: Have you stopped screwing since the first time you fantasized it? (*Laughter.*)

ROBERT LEA: Well, the French call the orgasm *le petit mort,* because after an orgasm it seems all complete, but you can still have it happen again.

M: That's why it's called "the little death." Because you can have another thousand more.

ROBERT LEA: Right. But each one of them takes something from you.

SARAH: Takes something from you?

JANE: Yeah, I don't understand that. And I don't understand how once you act out a fantasy it . . . I mean, you have to fuck a different way each time?

ROBERT LEA: No, no, no. With my wife, we go at it all kinds of ways, but having the forbidden fruit, the extramarital affair, that deserves some other excitement. I can be very excited. One can be, when a woman has an orgasm. . . .

M (*playing Robert Lea's alter ego*): "I would feel very ashamed of taking part in a two-man-one-woman thing."

ROBERT LEA: Not at all, not at all. As a matter of fact, I've already asked someone. (*Much general laughter.*)

YAEL: What happens to your best friend?

ROBERT LEA: He wanted this to happen. When he was still married to her, he told her about this. He liked it, he dug it.

SARAH: He liked having two people with his—?

BOB: Sharing his wife?

KARI: Oh, fuck it all. Why should always forbidden fruit taste the best?

ROBERT LEA: It does, baby. I don't know why, but it does.

KARI: Oh, shit.

ROBERT LEA: If women walked around the streets naked, I don't know if they would turn me on. If pot were legalized, I'd probably have to give it up.

KARI: Why doesn't Little Prince turn you on? Doesn't she?

ROBERT LEA: Not while I'm sitting here. She's so objective.

KARI: No. When you were across the room and looking at her.

ROBERT LEA: Yes. But you turn me on, too, doll.

KARI (*sarcastically*): Gee.

YAEL (*bewildered*): Why are you all so . . .

KARI: Now there is Little Prince, and she's sort of half-nudish. But if people walked around nude it would be no fun anymore. I'm just thrown out by that shit.

> At this point Little Prince jumps up and races from the room, screaming. She leaps over Marjorie's legs on the hall floor and dashes, still screaming, into the next room. Marjorie runs after her. She finds Little Prince on a couch, on her knees, facing the back. Over the couch back, a foot or so away, there is a partially opened window. Marjorie puts her arms around her and tries to soothe her.

LITTLE PRINCE (*continuing to scream, shriek, and sob*): It's horrible, it's horrible! I'm so dirty, dirty, dirty! I want to die! Let me die, let me die, LET ME DIE! ! !

M (*entering the room*): What's going on here?

MARJORIE: I'm afraid she'll jump or something.

M: What makes you think that?

MARJORIE: She says she wants to die.

M: You have a job to do. Go back in the hall and take notes.

MARJORIE: All right, but you stay with her.

M: If she jumps, it will have been her own decision. (*To Little Prince:*) Come back to the group and tell us about it.

LITTLE PRINCE: You don't want to hear anything I have to say!

M: I do. Honestly, I do. Whenever you control yourself, I'd like to have you come back in and talk to us.

> *Marjorie takes her old vigil in the hall. M returns to the group. Yael and Sarah both leave to help Little Prince but come back without solutions. At last Little Prince rushes out of the other office and leaves the apartment, slamming the door behind her. The following is recorded from the tape and begins at the time of the first screams:*

JANE (*worried*): Is she freaking out? (*She begins to follow Little Prince.*)

KARI: Stay put. Somebody's in there. Let's keep it in here, and that's that. Oh . . . why do I feel, like gosh, you know . . . that fuckin' razor's edge you can start walking on. I just can't stand the pain, I just can't stand the pain, I just can't stand the pain. . . . (*Her voice has dropped to a whisper.*)

BERNARD: What . . . ?

PHILIP: What kind of pain?

> *Throughout this Little Prince's screams are heard clearly by the group.*

KARI: Oh, just pain . . . just . . .

BERNARD: Just living?

KARI: Yeah . . . And just pain . . . and pain . . . and oh . . .

SCENE 5: KARI'S TRIP

SARAH: Do you feel we've hurt Little Prince?

KARI: Oh, no, no, no. Just being . . . If you want to be alive, the whole thing today is not to have to stand on things, right? Try to open up and get into everything? And some things are not easy to explain. They're rather painful. And for some people, it's more painful than others. Oh, I don't know. Sometimes it's not as painful on the outside as it is on the inside. I just switch it . . .

BERNARD: I don't get any sense of what she's saying. Does anybody else?

SARAH: What do you feel has happened?

KARI: That someone is feeling too much pain. Someone is feeling, and, and, and that feeling may be me, because I have a tendency of thinking a feeling, you know. I talk about the razor's edge. I mean when you're really in something. I mean, there's no joke about it. There's no talk about it. And I hate people talking, you know, once someone is all involved in something. . . .

JANE: You mean it's not worth it to open up?

KARI: It's frightening and scary to me. Maybe it's not worth it. . . .

SARAH: I don't know about you all, but I'm worried about what's happened to Little Prince.

M (*who has just returned*): If you're worried, go out and talk to her.

> *Sarah leaves the room.*

KARI: Oh, shit. I'm scared of this. It really gets me.

M: What?

KARI: When I feel someone is caught, it really gets me.

BERNARD: Because you identify? Do you feel like doing that yourself?

KARI: No, no. I would resist it, for my own protection.

BERNARD: It's funny, Kari—but I have a feeling that you're almost the only person here who hasn't really said what's bothering you. You keep talking in abstractions. Is it too painful to talk about?

KARI: I can't verbalize it. I don't know what in specific bothers me. . . . I react, I grab on. . . . (*She is sighing, struggling with words and feelings.*)

M: Kari, can you get up here and show us how you feel without talking? Put your body in the kind of position you think best shows your feelings.

> *She moves toward the center of the room, starts to take a position, then changes it. She seems indecisive, resigned, yet despairing, and looks upward, perhaps for some cue from on high.*
>
> *Now Sarah returns, with no verbal report of Little Prince.*

KARI (*suddenly close to tears*): Oh, God!

M: Don't talk.

BERNARD: Would you like to take a punch at somebody?

KARI: No.

M: Don't help her. Just let her do it with her body.

KARI (*shifting, sighing*): I'm dead. . . .

M: You're dead?

KARI: Yeah, I'm dead.

M (*taking a sheet from under the desk*): We'll bury you.

KARI: Like the song says, "Who's got the shovel . . . ?"

M (*covering her with the sheet*): If you're dead you've got to lie down.

> *Kari is now sitting on the floor, under the sheet. She moans and shifts about, looking and sounding like an agi-*

tated ghost. The moaning and the movements continue for two minutes.

M: How are you feeling now?

KARI: I don't want to fight.

M: What do you want to do?

KARI: I don't want to be awake again. I just want to be stoned....

M asks the others to lift Kari up in their arms and rock her. The group holds her prone, like a corpse, and begins to chant in unison: Ooommm, ooommm, ooommm. . . . After half a minute Kari, under her shroud, begins to sob—quietly at first, then louder. Then Kari starts to hum ooommm, ooommm, louder than the group. But soon her hum changes to a moan, and then to a distant ooohhh, emitted in a long expiration. This is followed by wracking sobs, all against a background of soft group humming. The atmosphere is solemn and funereal as nine people and M rock Kari back and forth, up and down, under her sheet. After three and a half minutes she is gently lowered to the floor.

M (*whispering*): Does everyone want to sit around and keep their hands on her?

Kari continues to sob.

M (*after another minute*): What's happening, Kari?

KARI (*in a voice choking with emotion*): I just can't, I just can't let go....

M: Let go. Let go again.

KARI: I can't.... It's like a curse....

M: What's a curse?

KARI (*sobbing again*): Your hands on me . . . It's like the hands that used to be on me a long time ago. . . . It was God, the hand of God, or the hand of the Devil....

M: Tell us more about it.

KARI: I can't stand the hand of God! Or the hand of the Devil! I'll resist it any day, any day!

M: You'll resist it any day?

KARI (*wailing*): I will! Out of principle, nobody can tell me anymore what to do, or fear. And guilt . . . Oh, it's like being possessed by nothing, and not being able to express it. . . .

M: What is it you want to express?

KARI: Pain.

M: Where does it hurt?

KARI: I hurt my finger. I want to feel the pain!

M (*taking Kari's finger, bending it back gently*): Like this?

KARI: Like that . . . but it doesn't really pain me. . . .

M (*applying more pressure*): Like this?

KARI: Now there's more pain there. . . .

> *M continues, slowly, to bend the finger back, until the pressure is forceful and extreme.*

KARI: Ouch!

M: Louder.

KARI: OUCH!

M: Still louder.

> *Kari screams another* OOWCH! *M keeps the pressure on, while she emits a series of long, agonized groans which soon turn to broken, jagged sobs.*

M (*softly*): What's happening now?

KARI: Oh, it makes sense now!

M: What?

KARI: Something makes sense anyway!

M: What makes sense?

KARI: Oh, the pain makes sense! And what happens afterwards makes sense if you allow it! And it doesn't make sense if you don't allow it. . . . (*She begins to get up from the floor and to shed the sheet.*)

M: Stay down.

KARI: No.

M: What's happening?

KARI (*sadly, unconvincingly*): Oh, it's okay now . . . it's fine.

M (*pushing her down*): Come on, it's not fine. (*He begins to twist her finger again.*)

KARI (*mixing laughter and tears*): Ouch! It's okay, Marty! Ouch! It's okay! It hurts, it hurts!

M: And what else hurts?

KARI: Everything hurts! Oh, God! It hurts to feel! It hurts to feel pain!

M: And what else?

KARI: And joy! And everything else! I've got to remember it now. . . . But I'm taking up time. I feel terribly selfish!

M: Is there something more you want from us? If you could have more time?

KARI: No, I don't want anything very nice . . . but it is very nice. . . .

M: So why do you want to stop it?

KARI: Well, that's the way I am. . . . Guilty.

M: What are you feeling guilty about?

KARI: I feel the way I usually feel by myself. But now I feel it with people around, too.

M: What way is that?

KARI (*who is sitting up now, without the sheet; she is looking down, her face wet with crying*): Oh . . . part of . . . people . . . involved . . .

M: You're not dead anymore?

KARI: I feel a little scared.

M: Scared of what?

KARI: People . . .

M: Do you want to look around at everybody? Do you want to tell them you're scared of them?

KARI (*looking at her audience for the first time*): No . . . no . . .

    M points to each member of the group separately, asking

Kari, "Are you afraid of her?"—"Are you afraid of him?"
Kari whispers soft nos.

M: Are you scared of me?

KARI: No.

M: Then who are all these people you're scared of?

KARI: I'm scared of me. I look at them, and I see me. And I don't like me. . . .

M: Do you want to tell us anything?

KARI (*sniffling*): I . . . it's hard for me just to feel your hand on mine, and just take from somebody . . . and . . .

M: Because what?

KARI (*beginning to cry again*): I . . . I . . .

M: Come on, let it out.

KARI (*sobbing*): It's not worth it! I'm not worth it!

M: Why aren't you worth it?

KARI: I'm no fucking good! A fucking curse on my shoulders! A fucking Black Angel behind me . . .

M: Can you tell us what a fucking shit you are?

KARI (*laughing now, speaking more lightly after the tears*): I remember one time when I was about eight my father said to me, "Ah, you went to the Tivoli!" And this fucking Black . . . he didn't say fucking . . . he said there was this Black Angel behind me. . . . Not that I'm looking around for a Black Angel, but there's this fucking curse. Because he was so fucking fanatic, you know. We would go to church, and it was so important, like Holy Rollers, and they put the finger of God on you. How dare anyone not feel it? I felt it into my shoes. Shame . . . shame . . . It was my father! Ah, God . . . And then I was laying in bed with my father, and all of a sudden I felt his leg, and his body moving . . . and then I just completely cut all my feelings off. But I got out of there, and I went to see my mother and my grandmother and told the story. But I didn't even know what was going on. I thought it had to do with masturbation, and everything.

And they're sitting there, and they're saying, "Oh, how horrible! How horrible of him!" And then I felt all this guilt.
. . . I didn't know what was happening . . . and I thought
maybe it was *my* feeling for *him* . . . and I feel ashamed that
I said he was no fucking good, I feel ashamed. . . . If anything, he was a cynical, hung-up fellow who couldn't help
himself. . . .

M: Is he dead now?

KARI: Yes, he's dead now.

M: Do you think he forgives you for saying that about him?

KARI: Yeah. I think so.

M: Yeah?

KARI: My father, may he rest, I know he forgives me.

M: Do you want to visit God and find out?

KARI: (*laughing*): I can't find out.

M: Listen, why don't you take a little trip, and we'll have you
visit God. Okay?

KARI: How are you going to arrange that?

M: Just lie down here. Lie on your back. Close your eyes. I
would like you to take a trip to heaven. Tell me when you
get there.

KARI (*on her back, eyes closed*): Once I wrote a story about how
I would go to heaven. . . .

M: Well, tell it to us when you get there. Are you there yet?

KARI: I've never made it yet.

M: Where are you?

KARI: In myself. I can't cross there anymore.

M: How did you get up there in the story?

KARI: I called it The Golden Sorrow. . . . It seems to be the in-
fluence of the Catholic . . . I was finally brought up a Catholic.

M: Tell it.

KARI: I can't see the face of God. But if I got up there, what would I be able to do except look down and see the people suffer?

M: What do you see?

KARI: Palm trees . . . a tree . . . sloping up, sort of, like a scoop . . .

M: Is your father there?

KARI: No, there's no one up there. Oh, I know I'll never make it into heaven. I don't want to go there, I don't want to make it. I don't know, Marty. I can't ever see him.

M: Can you see your father? Just look around the palm trees.

KARI: I can't see him.

M: Just watch for a palm tree, until you see him.

KARI: I see people . . . about a thousand people . . . People! Oh, don't hurt me!

M: What's happening now?

KARI: I'm on a road, and I'm all alone.

M: Can you start running down it as fast as you can? Keep running faster and faster until something happens.

KARI: I'm almost running . . . But I can't . . . I can't . . . It's just a feeling of something . . .

M: What feeling?

KARI: I can't!

M: Take it as far as you can.

KARI (sitting up): I can't . . . I just can't.

M: Now, what do you think all of these people here think of you?

KARI (looking around): Tell me what you think. . . .

M: Ask them specifically.

KARI (looking at Jane): Tell me what you think about me. . . .

JANE: I'm glad you cried. I wanted you to cry, and I was trying to cry, too. It was as if you were holding on, and holding on, and you had to let it go, and finally you let it go, and I was so glad you did.

M (to Kari): Look at her when she talks to you. You've got to

work hard to stay in contact, and that means looking at
people. Who else do you want to ask?

KARI (*nodding toward Shershonsky*): What do you think of me?

SHERSHONSKY: Well, now I think you're more open. Like it was
a very nice thing when you were c-crying. In a way, I felt
that was like me, I saw myself in it. I was hoping you'd let
loose, and you did, and even your face looks more relaxed
now. I hope you don't feel bad about yourself because I think
you helped yourself by doing it, and you helped me too, because I related to it. I was all shook up when you were
upset. . . .

M: Who else?

KARI (*looking at Sarah*): Please tell me . . .

SARAH: I felt a great deal of affection for you.

M: I think we all did.

SARAH: I feel like crying myself. (*She kisses Kari, and the two
women cry quietly together.*)

M (*to Kari*): It's pretty rotten, having someone kiss a rotten son
of a gun like you, isn't it?

KARI (*looking at Philip*): What about you?

PHILIP: I love you.

KARI (*weeping*): Oh . . .

PHILIP (*very gently*): I really do. I think we all do. You can
feel so much. . . .

SCENE 6: LITTLE PRINCE RETURNS

*Little Prince has let herself in through the front door,
which has been left unlocked. She comes down the hall
slowly, sadly.*

KARI (*seeing Little Prince as she enters the room*): Why don't you come here and cry with us? (*She half-laughs, half-sobs. The two girls meet at the center and embrace, tears in their eyes.*)

LITTLE PRINCE: What are you crying about?

KARI: I like to cry with you. (*The two break down, weeping audibly.*)

BERNARD: I don't know what you two cry so much about. I think I'm much worse off than either of you, and I didn't cry.

M: Do you want me to twist your finger, too?

BERNARD: No thanks.

SHERSHONSKY: Why shouldn't they cry? They're letting go.

KARI: It's good to cry!

BERNARD: How about having a good laugh together?

KARI: No. I'd much rather cry.

M: Tell him it's not a manly thing to do, it's infantile!

YAEL: No . . . but you'll get us all crying, and I don't think—

M: Anybody wants to join them, help yourself.

> *By now several others have begun to cry with Kari and Little Prince and seem to be enjoying it.*

BERNARD: I think this is indulging themselves too much.

KARI: Oh, shush you up!

M: Any one else's opinion you want?

KARI: No, I don't need it now.

M: Do you believe what these people said to you?

KARI (*laughing*): Yes, I do.

M: Do you really? A no-good shit like you?

KARI: Yes. I do.

M: A no-good shit like you who failed in a marriage, and did all those other terrible things? A Black Ghost haunting you . . . right?

KARI: Smile!

M: A smart aleck too, huh? Well, that's pretty bad.

KARI: But you're worse! You see, I can't see anything but myself in others, so I see one in you.

M: Uh-huh. I'll tell you something, though. I don't mind being a smart aleck. (*He laughs.*)

BERNARD: What are you crying about, Little Prince?

YAEL: I wanted to look for you. I'm g-glad you're back.

LITTLE PRINCE (*whispering through her tears*): I was in the park. Why did you cut me off?

M: I cut you off because I was tired of hearing about your body.

LITTLE PRINCE: I am too.

M: So I did us both a favor.

BERNARD: Did Marty hurt your feelings?

KARI: Well, he didn't hurt her finger.

SHERSHONSKY (*to Little Prince*): What do you care so much what Marty says?

LITTLE PRINCE: I got hurt. . . . I felt awful. . . . I was just trying to be honest! I was trying! (*She sobs.*) I thought maybe I could get it all over with. . . .

M: Get what over with?

LITTLE PRINCE: I thought I could clear it up once and for all. So you cut me off.

M: I'm tired of hearing about your body, though.

LITTLE PRINCE (*screaming*): Well, WHY DID YOU ASK ME TO COME HERE?

M: I asked you to come here to take part and learn something about yourself.

LITTLE PRINCE: That's what I was *trying* to do!

M: But you act like a fuckin' little princess, not a prince. No one's allowed to cut the little princess off.

LITTLE PRINCE (*beside herself with rage and anguish*): What am I to do? Is there some correct way to phrase it so you won't cut me off?

M: I have a right to cut you off. If you don't like it, tell me to shut up. You act like a little princess. I'm supposed to be perfectly enthralled by your whole thing about having the body of a model, and if it ever wears thin—wow!—you'll go out the window or into the park!

LITTLE PRINCE: No! I was asking you to help me!

M: How would I help you? Just let you go on being a little princess?

LITTLE PRINCE (*shrieking*): No! I want to clean me up!

M: There's a cake of soap in the bathroom.

LITTLE PRINCE: Very funny!

M: If you wanna clean yourself up so much, I don't know why you're copping out and running to the playground.

LITTLE PRINCE: Oh, I just want to die 'cause I can't make it! I can't make it! What am I doing that's so bad . . . ?

M: I don't know what you're doing that's so bad.

LITTLE PRINCE: I'm trying to get help! I came so far. . . .

M: Does "help" mean I'm supposed to love you, that everyone's supposed to love you?

LITTLE PRINCE: No!

M: Then what are you so pissed about?

LITTLE PRINCE: I can't get over this thing by myself!

M: So stick around. Don't run into the park when you feel bad.

LITTLE PRINCE: But I was trying, right then and there. . . .

M: Try harder.

LITTLE PRINCE: So if you were tired of hearing about my body, and you knew there had to be something more, why didn't you ask me what more there was?

M: I didn't feel like it at that point. Maybe Philip wants to hear about your body. You can always go out with him for five minutes.

LITTLE PRINCE: Very funny.

M: Why does everybody have to be enthralled by you?

LITTLE PRINCE (*sobbing softly*): I don't want people to be enthralled by me. . . .

M: Well, you're upset that I wasn't. If you stayed around here and gave up the histrionics you might learn something in the course of the evening.

LITTLE PRINCE: I'm trying to learn something.

M: Good. Now, does anybody else want to talk about a Shame?

ROBERT LEA: SCUM!

M: Do you want to take her side?

ROBERT LEA: I think she's a very beautiful person! Beautiful . . .

M: So I'm scum for talking to her that way?

ROBERT LEA: She's just weak to the blows you are constantly dealing on her.

M: Is that true? Are you that weak, Little Prince?

LITTLE PRINCE: I don't want to be weak. Like sometimes I'm very strong.

ROBERT LEA: You're very weak.

LITTLE PRINCE: I try. Jesus Christ, I try!

ROBERT LEA: You even cop out on yourself.

LITTLE PRINCE: I'll never get out of it. . . .

ROBERT LEA: Yes, you will. You came back, didn't you? You're halfway out, baby.

LITTLE PRINCE: But he did the same thing to me when I came back.

ROBERT LEA: But you're not reacting the way you did before. You were prepared for it. Prepare yourself. Everyone's going to bug you.

LITTLE PRINCE (frightened): Everyone's going to—?

JANE: Don't you feel like yelling at Marty, or hitting him or something?

The group shows approval. There are cries of "Do it, do it!"

LITTLE PRINCE: I've hit Art so many times. It's not going to make me feel any better. . . . And, hell, I don't hate Marty. I was just angry at him, and I don't—

M: Let's do something. You position us, like statues. You put

me into a position, the way you'd like me to be. Then put
yourself in one.

*She moves his head slightly with her hands; he is then
facing her directly, relaxed, without anger.*

BERNARD: The big problem with you two girls is that you both
think you're no fucking good.

LITTLE PRINCE: Well, it looks that way, doesn't it?

KARI (*beginning to cry again*): It does, doesn't it. . . .

LITTLE PRINCE: But I try!

M (*playing Little Prince's alter ego*): "Here I tried so hard, and
still he doesn't listen to me. Didn't I deserve a gold star for
all that effort?"

JANE (*also as Little Prince's alter ego*): "You're . . . you're a
prick. And I hate you. And I want to punch you. But I
think I can punish you more if I run away and cry."

M: Is that true?

LITTLE PRINCE: I wanted to hit you, but I'd rather go outside
and be like the Little Prince and lay down in the grass and
cry. . . .

SHERSHONSKY: Why don't you yell at him and say Fuck off, or
something?

LITTLE PRINCE: I still love him, in a way.

M: So that's how you'd like the relationship to be?

LITTLE PRINCE: Well, you don't mean drastically, do you . . . ?

M: Sure. Exaggerate. Make us into statues. Your ideal.

LITTLE PRINCE: I'd like to rap with you . . . I'd like to—

M: Don't say it. Position me how I'm supposed to be.

LITTLE PRINCE: I don't know. . . .

M: I'll give you thirty seconds.

LITTLE PRINCE: Oh, do I *have* to . . . ?

M: Now you have only ten seconds.

LITTLE PRINCE: I don't know how to put you! You don't have
to be anything! All you have to do is stop cutting me off!

M (*looking at his watch*): That's it.

LITTLE PRINCE: Okay.

M: Now, I'll give you another thirty seconds to put us into statues, the way we relate to each other.

PHILIP: Put him in it, Prince!

Little Prince continues to stall.

M: Another twenty-two seconds to go.

LITTLE PRINCE (*with a sob*): Okay! Stand up on something! High!

M: Put me on it.

> *She helps M to get on a chair. As he stands there, high above her, she moans and falls to the floor.*

ROBERT LEA: What is that? Worship?

LITTLE PRINCE (*shrieking*): NO! I did him as a PERSON!

ROBERT LEA: It's like idolatry.

LITTLE PRINCE: No! I dug everything he said today! I associated with it!

SARAH (*playing the alter ego*): "I'd certainly like to pull that chair out from under him, too!"

M: Is that true?

LITTLE PRINCE: Well . . . I don't particularly like people standing on chairs up above me.

M: You put me there.

LITTLE PRINCE: I guess I'm so mad . . .

M: You're getting what you want from me.

LITTLE PRINCE: What I really, really want is just for you to sit down and talk to me. You don't have to smile, and maybe it's even okay if you cut me off. I know I got upset about it, and I copped out . . . because . . . uh . . . well, when I was out there I wrote all those thoughts down. I can't remember some of them, but—

M: Anything else you want to do? If not, we're now going on to something else.

> *M has, tacitly, cut Little Prince off once more by ignor-*

ing her near-offer to look at, or read, some of the thoughts she wrote down while in the park.

There is no verbalization about this measure from the rest of the group.

Act 4: The Dominant-Passive Game

SCENE 1: THE LINEUP

M: Listen, we're going into the other room for this, where there's more space. I would like everybody to think about where they stand in terms of assertiveness and submissiveness. You know: how dominant you are, how passive you are. In the other room we're going to line up. Number One is the most assertive, the most dominant. Number Ten is the most submissive, or passive. After, we'll come back here and talk about it.

JANE: Including you?

M: Everybody but me.

YAEL: You mean where we stand in this particular group, or in life?

M: In this particular group of people. And no talking when we get in there.

> *The group goes off into the other room. The lineup begins, with M at the head, facing Number One. There is a great deal of physical jockeying, pushing, elbowing, and shoving. The competitors for first place are the roughest. Bernard seems to have the Number One position, until it is taken away by Robert Lea. Lea's strategy is stealth: He hugs M and gets the number-one spot*

while Bernard isn't looking. Jane makes a preliminary bid for a front position, but she retires toward the middle when the men prove more aggressive than she. Shershonsky allows himself the Number Ten position and refuses to contest anyone who wishes to stand ahead of him. Finally the lineup is established as follows:

1. Robert Lea
2. Bernard
3. Jane
4. Bob
5. Sarah
6. Philip
7. Yael
8. Kari
9. Little Prince
10. Shershonsky

SCENE 2: DISCUSSION

Back in M's office:

M: Now I'd like you to talk about what it was like for you as an experience, what you thought about, where you wound up, what you chose and why you chose.

ROBERT LEA: Uh, I'd like to say that when I chose the most assertive, the only one I knew I'd have any difficulty with was Bernard. (*To Bernard:*) Because you're the most visceral of us here, and I wasn't about to get into any scene, but I knew that I could con you. I think I knew that I'm more hip than you. Um . . . besides, I dig Marty's belly. (*Laughter.*)

CARL A. RUDISILL LIBRARY
LENOIR RHYNE COLLEGE

YAEL: I was annoyed, because out in life I would put myself immediately in front, but here I went toward the end.

ROBERT LEA: I would like to add that I am also the most yielding one here.

BERNARD: I think you're the most obnoxious. (*General guffaws.*)

JANE (*to Robert Lea*): You mean if he had yanked you out and put himself in front of you, you would have given up?

ROBERT LEA: Yeah. I mean I wasn't looking for a combat. It didn't mean that much to me. Depending on the situation, I would put myself last at times, but I thought it would be interesting to see if I belonged first. And Bernard didn't want to grab Marty around the waist. You know, that wasn't his scene. I mean, he would be a little bit startled at my . . . homosexual fantasy.

BERNARD: Yeah.

ROBERT LEA: You would never do that, and I knew it. And I had to find out if I could con you and make the move to first.

BERNARD: I think you're a little pushier than I am.

YAEL: I was surprised at Sarah. I would have expected Sarah even behind *me,* and there I saw her, very much in front. Oh . . . and it was very nice of you, Shershonsky, to be Number Ten.

BERNARD: It's not a question of being nice.

ROBERT LEA: Shershonsky wouldn't hurt anybody.

SARAH: Were you doing it to be a gentleman, or what?

SHERSHONSKY: No. I did it because that type of exercise represented to me a whole lot of shit. Bernard is out there in front with Robert Lea, and all that crap, and everybody's struggling to get ahead. That's the way life is, and that's a lot of shit. I don't like to compete. I'll fight anybody in the place for the last position. And if anybody—

M (*as Shershonsky's alter ego*): "I'll kill for last place, but I won't compete!" (*General laughter.*)

SHERSHONSKY: I won't go through the hassle. Like virility, hairy chest, Robert Ruark, Ernest Hemingway . . . A lot of shit. I, uh, don't go for this fighting, shoving, pushing, because I've been into that scene. I, uh . . . used to be a prizefighter. I used to get into the ring. I used to get knocked around when I was a kid. And I used to hit people. But it's just a lot of crap. And I don't like this structured kind of competition like you have in society—everybody trying to get to the head of the line.

BERNARD: Listen, I'd like to take issue with the point you're raising. Whether or not you think you're any better than the rest of us, or that we're more whorish than you are, has nothing to do with it. I'm not proud to have to try to fight for first place. But if I didn't, I wouldn't be playing the game according to the rules.

SHERSHONSKY: All right. I'll reverse it somewhat, as part of my problem. It's a thing about pushing to the head of the line, or wherever the hell you are. It's hard for me to do this.

ROBERT LEA: I would never push to get into the front of any line. I don't compete with anybody. Fortunately, I don't have to. I figured I'd just have to compete with Bernard.

SHERSHONSKY: This isn't a put-down of anybody here. It's just my problem. This is what's kept me from getting into certain things that I should have done for myself, and that I haven't done.

ROBERT LEA: You wound very easily, don't you?

SHERSHONSKY: Possibly.

ROBERT LEA: Yeah. Like you're such a nice guy, man.

SHERSHONSKY: I'm not that nice.

ROBERT LEA: If anyone got hurt here, you'd be very bugged. You'd make a very groovy, nice friend.

JANE: Taking it out of the context of a physical thing, do you think you're the most submissive person here?

SHERSHONSKY: No, I don't.

JANE: Then you were lying.

BERNARD: You don't like to get in and fight for a place in line. Why don't you say it?

SHERSHONSKY: It's a passive hostility kind of thing. . . .

BERNARD: . . . Honestly, I feel a little bit ashamed of the fact that I pushed to be Number One.

JANE: Why? Don't you feel that you're the most dominant person in the room?

BERNARD: I do feel that. At least I felt it before I met Robert Lea. (*Laughter.*)

JANE: So what do you feel ashamed of?

BERNARD: Because, uh, I don't like people who are overpowering, or overdominating. Just because I have these traits in me doesn't mean I have to admire it. I don't. (*To Shershonsky:*) But for you to feel that you're Number Ten, which may very well be your true place, doesn't necessarily mean that the other guys ahead of you are worse guys, or that they're willing to do something that you're too good for.

SHERSHONSKY: It's my problem. . . . I'm not saying—

BERNARD: Yeah. I mean this is just like life, in a sense. Nobody's any better than anyone else just because it happens that their own personality is a certain way.

PHILIP (*to Bob*): I was surprised at you. I had thought previously, "Well, I'll step out in front of him." And then I thought, "Wait a minute, if he's actually going to get up there, he's more dominant than me, and that's all there is to it."

BOB: That's funny, because my reaction was, "I'm probably just about where he is." So I started to walk over just in front of you, and then Sarah started pushing ahead, and I decided that I'm certainly more dominant than *her!*

BERNARD: Which girl was highest in line?

SARAH: Jane was.

BERNARD: That's right. Right behind me.

JANE (*to Philip*): Why didn't you fight me for Three?

PHILIP: I wasn't going to fight anyone for anything.

JANE: Oh, so you could have ended up Ten too.

M (*to Philip*): Your Big Brother would have hit you over the head, even if he was a little girl?

JANE: How many people didn't like it? Two people already are saying they didn't want to play the game.

SARAH: I enjoyed it.

BERNARD: M, where would you put yourself?

M: First or second. I did it once. I hid behind the little old lady who was first. (*Laughter.*) I figured I was pretty assertive, but I could never be the *most,* and some little old lady was there and I was holding on to her and keeping her first. (*More laughter.*) I think, in part, that that was my own shame, or embarrassment, about copping to the fact that I like to be first, or feel that I am without even wanting to be.

YAEL: I wonder if we had done the same thing this morning, if we would put ourselves in the same position. I think that this morning I would have tried to be at least second or third.

KARI: All I know is that I had to be behind you. I know that. And don't ask me why.

YAEL: Why behind *me?*

KARI: Well, because . . .

YAEL: Kari and I did it with smiles. First she was before me, but then I thought, "No, really, I have to be before her."

BERNARD: I think it might be interesting next time to have people, just by looking at each other, make up a list from One to Ten, including themselves.

M: You mean instead of First Impressions, do a Lineup?

Several people murmur assent.

SARAH: I just feel sort of self-satisfied, because I thought I could have predicted it—that either Robert or Bernard would be first, and that Jane would be third, and I thought I would be fourth. And then I thought Bob should probably be fourth. I didn't know whether he would struggle with me for it, but he did.

YAEL (*incredulously*): Jane was before you?

SARAH: Yeah.

YAEL: You didn't want to be before her? Because when I saw you struggling—

SARAH: No, no. I thought Jane and the men should be ahead. And I thought Bob should probably be ahead, but if I were presumptuous enough, he might not challenge me. But he did. (*She laughs.*)

YAEL (*to Bob*): Did you push her, or did you tickle?

SARAH: He was pushing, he was really pushing, and I was really trying, but, you know . . . I . . . (*A long pause.*)

> *Philip suggests a new lineup in which each person positions himself without fighting. M agrees to this, but the result is a good deal of milling about, ending up with positional dissatisfactions and no real solution.*

LITTLE PRINCE: What would have been good, perhaps, is that if three people thought they should have been first, they should have lined up in a parallel line.

YAEL: It's a real problem because I'm very much influenced by . . . by the hur-hurting of fingers, and so forth.

BERNARD: I think the most important thing is the relationship between where you think you stand, and where other people think you stand. That's why I'd like to see everybody make out a list.

M: What do these positions have to do with the way you live your lives?

LITTLE PRINCE: Well, first, I was against the idea of competition. And the second thing was that at the same time as knowing something about myself, I also didn't know about myself. The third thing was that I didn't know where I wanted to go, so I felt more or less lost. And perhaps not knowing equals being lost, equals copping out, and that might say something about what I did before, and being negative. Then the fourth thing is that I guess I must have been affected by what I did before. . . .

SARAH: Earlier in the day, when we were doing First Impressions, where would you have put yourself?

LITTLE PRINCE: I felt great. I would have been Number One.

YAEL: Ah, I wouldn't have let you be Number One! (*The women laugh.*)

Act 5: Personal Ratings

SCENE 1: BERNARD'S OBNOXIOUSNESS

BERNARD: I'll tell you what I'm most concerned with—my shtick, hang-up, whatever it is—and I think everybody shares this to some degree . . . the, uh, comparison between what I think of myself and what other people think of me.

M: How would the comparison be graded?

BERNARD: What I'm interested in is: Am I correct in my interpretation of how I come on to people?

BOB: Doesn't this contrast with what you were saying at the beginning, when you wanted to overcome your preoccupation with how people felt about you? You said this morning that one of the things that bothered you was the fact that it bothered you if people didn't like you.

BERNARD: Yes, it bothers me that it bothers me.

M: What do you want to ask us now? About what qualities?

BERNARD (*after a long pause*): Do you think, uh, for example . . . that I'm extremely obnoxious? Very obnoxious . . . ?

THE GROUP (*in chorus*): Don't, don't, don't!

BERNARD: Wait . . . wait a second. I have the floor. I have a right to ask these questions and I'm not being silly either. I'm quite serious. Do you think I'm very, uh . . . extremely obnoxious, very obnoxious, mildly obnoxious, not particularly obnoxious, or not obnoxious at all?

M: Who are you asking?

BERNARD: I'm asking Jane.

JANE: Not at all.

BERNARD: Not at all?

BOB: I would say, uh . . . moderately.

YAEL: Uh, to me you don't seem obnoxious at all, but I don't like the-the-the way of categorizing. I would rather if you would ask me am I *simpatico* to you, or how do I feel toward you.

BERNARD: I'm not asking that, though. I'm asking a particular thing. Everybody knows what an obnoxious person is.

YAEL: You don't seem to me obnoxious.

BERNARD: Um . . . Shershonsky?

SHERSHONSKY: Straight out? No qualifications?

M: Right.

SHERSHONSKY: Obnoxious. Medium.

PHILIP: Not at all.

LITTLE PRINCE: I think you can come on as that, but I don't think you are.

PHILIP: You qualified it.

LITTLE PRINCE: I know.

BERNARD: It's probably that people who ask questions like this . . . well, it's an obnoxious question to begin with. (*Laughter.*)

YAEL: Of all the things, why don't you ask if-if-if you are sexually attractive?

BERNARD: I'm coming to that. (*Much laughter.*)

KARI (*shrieking loudest of all*): Don't worry, he'll get there!

YAEL: Why, from all the things, to come out with obnoxious?

BERNARD: It must be something that concerns me.

ROBERT LEA: It obviously concerns you! Well, you're not obnoxious, but you like to come on like gang-busters.

KARI: What are the categories again?

BERNARD: Very, moderately, mildly, and not at all.

KARI: Not very.

BERNARD: Mildly?

KARI (*laughing*): Oh, you *know* you're obnoxious!

ROBERT LEA: Why are you so unsure of yourself?

BERNARD: I don't know.

M: I don't find you obnoxious.

BERNARD: That's very interesting.

M: What does it all mean to you?

BERNARD: Well, about half the people here think I'm at least mildly obnoxious, and half the people don't think I'm obnoxious.

M: No. About eighty percent thought you were not particularly obnoxious, and twenty percent did.

BERNARD: Shershonsky thought I was obnoxious.

KARI: Does it imply to you that people don't like you because you're obnoxious? I don't mind people who are obnoxious.

BERNARD: But by definition that means that I irritate, that I—

KARI: I don't agree with that.

M: Are you surprised?

BERNARD: Um . . . I would have expected more people would find me obnoxious.

M: So they didn't. So what does that mean to you?

BERNARD: If we did this with a blind ballot, I think I would get a higher obnoxious rating.

ROBERT LEA: What do you want to be so obnoxious for? You are so fucking defensive, man, that you want everybody to think you're obnoxious!

BERNARD: No . . . I *don't* want everyone to feel I'm obnoxious.

M: Would you believe in it more if we did a hidden ballot?

BERNARD: Yeah. I want everybody to write it down. You know.

KARI: Why, why, Bernard . . . why does it really mean that much to you?

BERNARD (*with annoyance*): Look, I listened to you cry for about half an hour!

KARI: Right, right.

BERNARD: So you can listen to *my* hang-up.

KARI: We laid on top of you for I don't know how long!

SARAH: Ah, let's not fight over things that are petty!

ROBERT LEA: Yeah, let's get on with this thing.

M: Okay, we'll vote Severely, Mildly, or Not. And you try to guess how the ballots are going to come out.

BERNARD: I want everybody to be truthful.

There is much chatter and giggling as M passes out pencils and paper and tells them to abbreviate the votes with S, M, and N.

YAEL (*as the ballots are being collected by Jane*): Anybody want a candy? I'm going out for a candy.

M: Do you want Jane to open them, Bernard, or do you want to open them?

SARAH: You open them, Bernard.

Jane hands them to Bernard.

SARAH: Yeah, that's better.

BOB: And we want an honest count.

BERNARD: I'll just shuffle them up a little bit. . . .

SHERSHONSKY: He's going to stuff it with Severelies!

M: Okay, loud and clear now.

SARAH: I'm the poll-watcher.

BERNARD (*opening the ballots and reading aloud*): Mildly obnoxious. Not obnoxious. Not obnoxious. Mildly obnoxious . . . Not obnoxious . . . Not obnoxious. Mildly obnoxious . . . Not obnoxious . . . Not obnoxious . . . Not obnoxious.

SHERSHONSKY: You lose! (*Uproarious laughter.*)

BERNARD: I don't know. . . .

M: You got seven for Not, three for Mildly, and none for Severe.

M then looks at the slip of paper on which Bernard has written down his own guesses, which reads: five Nots, three Mildlies, and two Severelies.

M: You guessed that two people would vote you Severely Obnoxious, and nobody did.

BERNARD: Yeah.

M: Now what does that mean to you?

BERNARD: It means, obviously, that I think I'm more obnoxious than other people think I am. This is an interesting insight. . . .

M: How do you feel about it? Better?

BERNARD: Yeah. I feel sort of like it's a little bit of a vote of confidence.

SARAH: I don't know if that's true. As I was sitting here I was sure you were going to cheat on the side of obnoxious, and that's why I was watching.

SHERSHONSKY: I hope this doesn't encourage you to further efforts, Bernard.

> *Bernard seems bewildered by the vote, while Kari laughs loudly and hysterically.*

BERNARD (*blushing, smiling sheepishly*): May I keep these ballots?

> *There is general good-hearted laughter.*

BERNARD: In case anybody ever tells me I'm obnoxious I can show them these votes. I have proof that the votes were seven to three! (*He joins in the laughter.*)

YAEL: Did you hear what Shershonsky said?

BERNARD: What?

SHERSHONSKY: I said I hope this won't encourage you to further efforts.

ROBERT LEA: What do you think of the capabilities of those of us who judged you? Do you think it's worthwhile?

BERNARD: I think the people here are a fairly good cross section of the type of people who I deal with ordinarily. But you seem surprised that I should be interested in this.

M: No, I'm not surprised.

BERNARD: I misinterpreted your feeling, then.

M: On what basis?

BERNARD: I thought you were reluctant to go into this.

M: Oh, no. I was trying to find out what it meant to you; whether you'd be freer about doing your thing with people. After all, you were telling us about some terrible sexual fantasies, your terrible aggressive qualities, and all that other stuff. You know, you're not usually an open person (*Bernard nods*) and yet you've been pretty open in doing a number of things. I was wondering if you wouldn't believe the votes and think we were kidding you. How does it appear to you?

YAEL: You don't think we were not honest!

BERNARD: No, there's no reason why you shouldn't be. The only rules of this whole game are honesty.

BOB: But you didn't believe it when we did it verbally.

BERNARD: I, uh, felt it might be, uh, difficult. . . .

M: It was about the same, verbally.

BERNARD: Yes . . . it was.

M (*smiling at Bernard*): Do you want to give a speech, or thank people, or jump up and down and yell Yippee?

SCENE 2: HOW SEXY AM I?

BERNARD: How many . . . uh . . . how many of you girls think I'm sexy? (*He blushes.*)

YAEL (*laughing*): I'm so glad you asked because that's the only question that really interests me, but I don't care to ask it about *me*.

BERNARD: Well, let me just put it into categories. . . .
     Sarah and several others moan. This is followed by laughter, particularly Yael's.

M (*shouting above the noise*): Severely Sexy! Mildly Sexy! Not Sexy at All!

YAEL: You mean how many years on an island if I would be alone with him?

BERNARD: Okay, do it this way: Someone who thinks I'm sexy but they wouldn't go out of their way to have an affair with me; sexy to the point where they *might* go out of their way, if the circumstances were right, to have an affair with me; and third—wouldn't even bother to have an affair with me if the circumstances *were* right.

YAEL: A long affair?

SHERSHONSKY: One night.

YAEL: Well, I was just sort of thinking . . .

JANE: You decide *beforehand?*

YAEL: No, but . . .

BERNARD: The length would depend on how I perform the first time, right?

KARI: Oh, shit!

JANE: No, I want to answer this. I'd give you a Number Two.

M: All right, Jane gave you a Number Two: Yes, if the circumstances were right.

JANE: But I wouldn't go out of my way.

BERNARD: Oh.

KARI: Oh, boy!

Yael asks Bernard to stand up. He does, and she looks him over with the same care one might show in the buying of a horse. The group laughs.

YAEL: I would like you slimmer, but I agree with Jane. I give you Number Two.

SARAH: I'd go out of my way for you. Number One.

BERNARD: Yeah?

SARAH: Yeah. I feel you're real attractive.

LITTLE PRINCE: Maybe I'd desire him if I didn't have hang-ups, and maybe I'd desire him anyway. Number One.

KARI: Gee, you know you don't appeal to me sexually at all.

BERNARD: That means zero, then.

KARI: Yeah. You don't appeal to me.

ROBERT LEA: I think you're a Number Two, if the situation would ever arise. (*Laughter.*)

M: How do you feel, Bernard?

BERNARD: Um . . . I'm left with a vague feeling of disappointment and Kari has put me down so.

M: And what about the rest?

BERNARD: The rest . . . ? Uh . . . it pleases me, of course, but . . . but it really disturbs me to find someone who—

SARAH: Four girls have rated you One or Two, and all you do is focus on the other one!

YAEL: Yes. We feel very rejected that our vote of confidence has just been thrown out the window.

BERNARD: Yeah. Well, but I'm not trying to please you people. I'm just trying to tell you that I'm left with a vague feeling of disappointment.

M: You always tend to exaggerate the negative.

BERNARD: Yeah, that's probably true.

YAEL: I . . . I-I-I would like to know also. About me. Would anyone go out of their way? Would they not go out of their way?

M: Do you want to ask all the guys whether they'd give you a One, Two, or Three for sexiness?

YAEL (*blushing, hesitating*): Uh . . . no. . . .

M: I'd give you a Two-minus.

PHILIP (*chivalrously*): Not a Two-and-a-half?

M: No. I would not go out of my way. If the situation were right, I might. I don't find you distasteful, Yael, but I would not pursue it.

ROBERT LEA: I would think, uh . . . that it's conceivable that you would turn me on. If the opportunity came, uh . . . I would at least hope that it would be mutually satisfying.

BERNARD: I'd give you a Two.

PHILIP: I'd give you a Three.

SHERSHONSKY: I would, uh, say Three.

BOB: I think I would say Three, but for very personal reasons. I think I would give a Three to anyone in the room.

M: Ah hah!

BOB: But it would have nothing to do with any of *you!*

PHILIP: Why not forget that you're married? It would be more interesting.

JANE: Yeah.

SARAH: I'd like to know, too. About myself.

M: I'd probably give you a Two-plus.

SARAH (*her eyes picking up*): Hhhmmnn.

M: It's conceivable that I could see you in terms of a One, except that you're so quiet, and it would never occur to me that you'd want it.

ROBERT LEA: Your eyes are very expressive, and I think that I could see you in terms of a One.

BERNARD: I'd give you a Two.

PHILIP: So would I.

SHERSHONSKY: One-minus.

BOB: I have to say Three.

ROBERT LEA: You're really tuned out!

BOB: Yeah.

SARAH: Well, I'm surprised, because I'd have rated myself lower.

BERNARD: You're not interested, Kari, in being rated?

KARI: No.

ROBERT LEA: Bernard, you have a thing with Kari, right? She turns you on, doesn't she? You'd give her a Number One, wouldn't you?

BERNARD: Yes, I would. You're not interested either, Little Prince?

LITTLE PRINCE: No.

BERNARD: Because you don't want to hear?

ROBERT LEA: She's afraid.

M: How would you rank her, Bernard?

BERNARD: One.

M: I think you were looking for an opportunity to tell Kari and Little Prince that they're very groovy chicks, but you didn't want to do it straight, so you asked them if they wanted to have you rate them.

BERNARD: Yeah. Well, I just can't come out and say it.

ROBERT LEA: Yes, you can!

KARI: Why can't you?

ROBERT LEA: Do it, do it!

LITTLE PRINCE: He already has, by the things he's done all day.

M: He walked over and sat down next to Kari a while back, when I said people should do what they wanted to do. Listen . . . do you want to rank the same sex now?

SARAH: What do you mean? Uh . . . do you mean which women I think would be attractive? How they would be attractive to men, you mean?

M: Who you think of as sexiest.

KARI: What man I think is the sexiest, or what woman?

> *The rest of the group remains silent. This is the first incidence of either incomprehension or unconscious withdrawal.*

M: Forget it.

Act 6: Take a Risk

SCENE 1: A BUILDUP OF COURAGE

M: What I would like you to do now is think of something you could do that would be a risk for you. And what I mean by a risk is that when you think of it, you get a really queasy, tense feeling in your gut.

JANE: Do it, or say it?

M: Whatever it is: If it's a doing-thing, do it; if it's a saying thing, say it; and if it's a solitary thing, perform it alone.

> *There is a very long silence, punctuated here and there with expressions of hesitance and uncertainty. While the marathon itself is a risk-taking experience in human relationships, this pinning down of daring on an individual basis seems to evoke a good deal of fear. The hush which drops upon the room indicates that the participants are, silently, going through a series of possible choices and rejecting many of them.*

M (*finally*): All right now, what brave soul will start?

SARAH: The risk for me is in saying it, not doing it. I'd like to wrestle with some guys. . . .

M: Why don't you just approach some guy and start wrestling?

> *Sarah chooses a rematch with Shershonsky. Her arm is quickly pinned to the floor.*

SARAH: As I said, it was more a risk to say it than to do it.

M: Why was it a risk to say it?

SARAH: Uh . . . I feel embarrassed that somebody should know that I'd want to do it with them. And, uh . . . I'm also a little afraid that it might have seemed sexual.

JANE: Did you want to stop at wrestling?

SARAH: I wanted to do something that was physical.

JANE: Yeah. For *now*. . . .

SARAH (*defensively*): I wanted to do something like . . . you know, where my body would get stretched in some way. I was tired of sitting on a chair.

JANE: Did it get stretched?

SARAH: Yes. I didn't want to screw with him now, if that's what you meant.

> *Shershonsky performs his risk next. He takes Jane out into the hall and kisses her. As they return to the room, he embraces her once more.*

M: How was that a risk for you?

SHERSHONSKY: Two ways. Uh . . . possible rejection is a risk. And the other thing is . . . well, you know it's not easy for me . . . like sort of to kiss a girl. Some people kiss very easy. You go somewhere, somebody kisses your wife, everybody is kissing. I don't do that too easy because, you know, if I hold someone or touch them, it feels good and it's nice. And that's a kind of threatening thing because it can open you up.

M: What's the risk in being opened up?

> *Shershonsky tries to explain that if he finds kissing girls pleasurable he may also discover that he isn't quite as satisfied with his wife as he may have thought he was. This, he says, could cause a lot of trouble.*
>
> *M suggests that while this might be true, Shershonsky might, by getting into closer touch with his sexuality through other women, be able to carry some of the rewards home to his wife and become more turned on to*

her. It sounds like an interesting idea to Shershonsky,
but he is not wholly convinced.
Bob's risk is to tell M and the group that he doesn't like
the way things have been going for the past hour or so.
He says that he has been left out of things, that the
group feeling seems to be dissipating because the focus
is now shifting toward individual hang-ups. When asked
why it is a risk for him to express this opinion, he says
that he's afraid everyone else is going to disagree with
him.

M (*good-naturedly*): How about if I get up and slug you for daring to criticize me?

BOB (*in all seriousness*): It's not the risk of any physical violence as much as a feeling of group pressure, of people saying, "Well, that's a funny kind of opinion." I mean, I feel maybe there's something wrong with me if nobody else feels this way.

LITTLE PRINCE: Do you know that nobody else feels this way?

BOB: No. Maybe I should ask that.

LITTLE PRINCE: Yeah.

BOB: How many people are dissatisfied with the way things have been going for the last hour or so?

LITTLE PRINCE: I'm not enjoying it. I'm not happy. But like right now what M wants us to do is very good because I'm having a hard time. I'm coming to something and it could be good for me.

JANE: I don't see any big difference between now and before.

YAEL: I feel a difference, but I'm not dissatisfied. I-I-I feel it was necessary to take this step to what we are now doing.

SARAH: I feel kind of anxious, and uh . . . uncomfortable inside, and not really into anything with anybody.

SHERSHONSKY: I feel a little keyed up, like I'm tuned into everything very carefully, and it feels kind of good. I think more things are happening now than happened before.

M: How do you feel standing alone, Bob?

BOB (*after a long pause*): I don't feel the way they do.

M: Yeah? How do you dare? Nobody else agreed with you. You must be crazy.

Bob and M continue to argue, M with prods and jibes. In the end Bob is left with his opinion, looking and sounding extremely uncomfortable. As Yael points out, it does not occur to him to tell M that Sarah actually did agree with him.

BERNARD: I'm getting terrifically bored with this. I'll tell you the risk I'd like to do. I'd like to take Little Prince into the other room and make a little bit of light love to her.

Bernard and Little Prince leave.

Philip's risk is to express his desire to turn on with pot. He feels that his asking for this may alienate a few of the people. Actually, he wants the pot so that he will be able to open up a bit more and heighten his perceptions in the group relationship; but the risk is not performable because there is no pot on the premises to give him.

Jane's risk is to kiss M. Her fear echoes that of Shershonsky. She believes that in kissing M she may become less satisfied with her lover, David. When the risk has been taken she is remarkably relieved to find that she loves David as much as ever.

SCENE 2: BERNARD'S NORMALCY

Bernard returns to the room with Little Prince.

M: Why don't you tell us, Bernard, what happened when you were outside with Little Prince, and how it was a risk for you.

BERNARD: Well, I took her into the other room and I kissed her, and fondled her. It was a risk, because I'm usually too inhibited. I don't ever recall just doing what I felt like doing. And I might have been rebuffed, or people might think I was just taking advantage of her, and that would make me feel very guilty.

ROBERT LEA: You almost lifted her up bodily and took her out. You didn't even give her a chance to rebuff you.

JANE: I find it hard to believe that you've never done what you felt like doing with women before.

BERNARD: Well, this was one of my fantasies: to see someone attractive and take them into the next room, and make love to them. I feel like this all the time, but I never do it.

M: And they don't have to be big, black, three-hundred-pound women? (*Laughter.*) Well, suppose she had rebuffed you. So what?

BERNARD: Oh, I would have been enormously embarrassed. It would be very painful for me. I might even leave.

KARI (*laughing loudly and with great mockery*): God, you're at the mercy of everybody! I thought I was in trouble, but baby —you're in greater trouble! Oh, what a poor, insecure, obnoxious person you are!

BERNARD: Does anybody *not* mind being rejected?

JANE: Nobody likes being rejected, but I wouldn't walk out and leave this whole thing if somebody rejected me.

M: Bernard, you could have had five minutes out of the room, but you came back in one minute. Did you think if you kept her out there any longer she'd have rejected you?

BERNARD: Yes. You're probably right. . . .

KARI (*jeering*): If he stayed longer he would be rejected!

M: Little Prince, would you have allowed him to stay outside longer with you if he had persisted?

LITTLE PRINCE: Surely.

Everyone begins to laugh, Kari the loudest.

BERNARD (*laughing with them*): I'm a real loser!

M: The thing is, that's what always happens if you feel it's going to be such a terrible, obnoxious disaster if somebody turns you down. Rejection is just going to happen sometimes in this world. But you're afraid, so you miss out on opportunities to have pleasure. You just blow your chances for happiness.

BERNARD: Yeah. Maybe this is a good lesson.

KARI (*cackling loudly*): You're a bridge-burner, you are! You just take all the chances away from yourself!

BERNARD: Uh . . . do you think I behaved in a . . . that what I did was not normal?

M: You're back on your normal kick now.

BERNARD: I mean is there something wrong with what I did, coming back so soon?

M: It was not normal.

BERNARD: It was not normal?

M: No. It was not normal.

YAEL: Bernard! Don't let him push you into a corner!

ROBERT LEA: He pushes himself into a corner.

KARI (*screaming*): He sure does! He's got his foot on his head!

BERNARD (*slowly, deliberately*): I daresay that every male here would like to take Little Prince in the other room and lay her. But so far I'm the only one who's gotten up and done anything with her. So you're talking about that I'm not normal, and yet, so far, I've done more than anybody else here. So you see, by definition, an operational definition of normality is—

He is drowned out by laughter.

BERNARD (*continuing*): —so I'm in the top one percent.

M: But normal men *don't* do what they feel like doing. Normal men are so afraid of being rebuffed that they would never do it.

BERNARD: So what did I do wrong? I didn't stay long enough?

M: That was perfectly normal.

BERNARD (*failing to catch on*): So you agree. I'm normal.

M: Right. So now you're happy stopping after one minute, because now you know you're normal.

BERNARD: Yes. In that sense, I'm happy.

M: A normal man wouldn't have gone out, but if he had, he'd have come back in one minute. Are you happy being a normal man?

BERNARD: Yes. I would be very unhappy if I, uh . . . got up and took Robert Lea into the other room even if that would have gratified me. But, uh . . . I'd feel unhappy because then I . . . I would not be normal. There's a certain gratification that one gets out of being just normal, being *considered* normal.

SARAH: Even if it's distressing?

M: You want to be a normal man or do you want to be your *own* man?

BERNARD: Uh . . . I want to be both.

M: Suppose you can't be both. The normal man is just a compilation of statistics. The average man.

BERNARD: I don't want to be the average man.

M: That's the normal man, isn't it?

BERNARD: The normal man is heterosexual. I want to be heterosexual.

M: What do you mean, you *want* to be? *Aren't* you?

BERNARD: Yeah. Well, listen . . . is it the group's feeling that I am not, well . . . I won't say normal . . . I'll say a healthy male. Is that the group's feeling?

BOB: I think you're a little foolish.

ROBERT LEA: You're just not freaky enough.

SARAH: I don't think normal people are healthy.

JANE: And I don't think you took a fantastic risk anyway.

LITTLE PRINCE: I agree.

ROBERT LEA: Yeah, what kind of risks were involved? I can't see any risks.

BERNARD: If you can't, then why don't *you* do it?

ROBERT LEA: All right, all right. I'll ask Little Prince to go out-side with me and allow myself to be rejected.

M: Is that your risk, Robert Lea?

ROBERT LEA: Well, what I'd really like to do is ask Jane to go outside with me. Jane's rejection would really be a risk for me.

M: Ask her.

ROBERT LEA: Jane, will you go outside with me?

JANE: No.

ROBERT LEA (*quietly*): Well, that's it.

M: How are you feeling?

ROBERT LEA: Um . . . not too badly. (*He begins to laugh and is joined by the others.*)

JANE (*to Bernard*): It wasn't a risk for you, really. First, before, you said you thought I'd be a good lay. Then you were in-terested in Kari and Little Prince. But I think of the three of us, you asked Little Prince because you sensed that she was the one with whom there was the least chance of rejection.

LITTLE PRINCE: That could be. . . .

BERNARD: Well, now, what one does is add up the percentage of gratification and then subtracts from that the—

KARI (*shrieking again*): Shit! You just turn me off! You *are* obnoxious, Bernard!

BERNARD (*stolidly*): I was just rationally figuring my chances of rejection. The chances of rejection from Kari would have been eighty percent. My percentage-opportunity with Little Prince would have been—

KARI: Oh, Jesus!

M: I want to say something to Bernard. You've got to think a lit-tle more about your quest for normalcy. Because you're tying yourself up in knots. You're cutting off what you want to do because it may be bizarre. The normal man doesn't live very much, you know. He doesn't get out of life as much as he can.

BERNARD: Are you saying that I ought to do whatever I feel like doing?

M: More of it, certainly. More of it.

YAEL (*incredulously*): In the real world?

M: Yes, absolutely.

YAEL: I agree more with Bernard. In the real world to get re-buffed would be very painful.

M: If you're as caught up with the fear of rebuff as he is, you're putting yourself in the same position, cutting yourself off. Aren't you the one who wants a lover all the time?

YAEL: That's just talk. But yes . . . yes . . . by being so worried about how do people look at me, and am I too short, and am I not pretty enough, I-I-I don't take the risks that could bring me gratification. . . .

M: Bernard, listen: Carry those votes around in your pocket, and the next time you find someone you like, if they give you the cold shoulder, whip out the votes and look at them, and stay longer. You're starving yourself, I think.

> *There is a chorus of yesses and yeahs from the others.*

ROBERT LEA: Gee, I really feel for you! You know, there's a whole *world* out there!

SCENE 3: YAEL'S TRIP

M: Yael, were you going to do a risk?

YAEL: I can't decide of three things which was the one I wanted to do.

JANE: Do the one that makes you most uncomfortable.

SARAH: Do them all.

> *The others shout encouragement. Yael, giggling, goes over to M and positions him so that an embrace is possible.*

YAEL: Lean back. Sit, sit, sit. Put your arms around . . . Turn that microphone off! (*Laughter.*)

PHILIP: Hey, that's great!

LITTLE PRINCE: Yeah!

YAEL (*snuggling in M's arms, without kissing him*): Mmmmm, that's nice. . . . (*Then she steps away.*)

BERNARD: If it's so nice, why are you stopping?

M (*amid general laughter*): Good question, Bernard!

YAEL: I was wondering . . . I want once to experience that thing in the air, like Kari. But I'm very scared that I would get some feelings that I don't want. . . .

M: You want us to rock you?

YAEL: Yes . . . but then I think how Kari cried so, and I think that instead of feeling very good it might make me feel very bad. . . .

M: Come on, lie down and close your eyes.

YAEL: With the sheet, too?

M: No, I don't think so. Do you?

YAEL: Uh . . . no.

> *Yael lies down on the floor and closes her eyes. The group lifts her up in its collective arms, softly humming the word "*OM*." They rock her for about three minutes and then put her down. At this point everyone is silent except Kari, who begins to hum a strange three-note tune: a high note, a low note, and then a middle note. She goes on, lost in her own melody, until M motions for her to stop so that Yael can come back to reality.*

YAEL (*still lying on the floor, eyes closed*): That was very good. I could relax. Usually when I lie in bed or when I do something my muscles are extremely tense. But that was a very good experience. It was a very eerie feeling. I never had that before. Only now I think that I don't have the right to take everybody's attention like that. . . .

M: Do you want to say more about it?

YAEL: No, not really. . . .

M: Do you want to say more about the eerie feeling? Where in your body did you feel it?

YAEL (*laughing nervously*): Where-where-where I'm supposed to feel it.

M: Where are you supposed to feel it?

YAEL (*motioning to her groin*): Right here. It was a very, uh . . . sexual feeling. Uh . . . if I would dream of a very ideal lover, I would think that this is what it should be like. . . . I-I-I thought for many years in my first marriage that I was frigid. I-I-I didn't know there was such a thing as an orgasm. When I listen to the younger people, I think, "How lucky they are! They don't have to go through this horrible torture of thinking that you do it only the 'right' way, never touching the, uh . . . clitoris, or with fingers." I wasted years thinking that way. This generation can speak out about it, and even with hang-ups, which I have seen today, they are much luckier than people my age or older who-who-who don't get that feeling at all. I feel that I must move fast to fulfill all those years that I missed out.

M: Uh-huh.

YAEL: It's . . . it's very interesting that when I talk about sex things, I still keep that smile on my face, like a mask. Very often I don't talk about what happened to me in my childhood, because . . . because I know that it hurts me to do it, and I know it hurts others. I-I-I try to smile upon it. On the one hand, I don't want to provoke pity; on the other hand, I feel a certain pride of having gotten out of it what I did get.

JANE: How are you feeling now?

YAEL: I would like someone to hold my head up a little.

KARI (*taking Yael's head in her hands*): I'd like to do it.

YAEL: Well, since we are talking honestly, I-I-I think I should get it out: Both my parents were killed in Auschwitz, which is a concentration camp, and, uh . . . I've had a lot of trouble feeling guilty by being alive while so many other kids and Jews were killed . . . were killed. But it's something that I manage somehow. I don't know what gave me the strength, but I managed to live with it. But from time to time it bothers me, and-and-and it could very well be that this didn't allow me to . . . to enjoy sex. It took a long time until I realized that a clitorical orgasm *is* an orgasm, not something that is wrong. . . .

M: What else would you like?

YAEL: Uh . . . you could kiss me.

M (*after kissing her gently on the mouth*): How do you feel your folks would feel about what you're doing now if they were alive?

YAEL: Well, actually they would be very disappointed. I'm in my third marriage and wanting to kiss other men. I guess they would turn in their grave, if they had a grave. But with my children, they would be delighted. I feel very often very sad that my children do not have grandparents; and sad for myself, too, not being able to show my mother and my father what I have done.

M: How old were you when they died?

YAEL: I was sent out of Germany when I was ten, from luck, but uh . . . usually with my friends and my business associates, I do not bring it up.

M: Do you remember your parents?

YAEL: I waited for many years, about fifteen. There were lists coming out of Germany of survivors. Not only myself, but some other kids used to wait for this list to see if the names were on it. I was an only child of my parents. Uh . . . it was pretty gruesome. . . .

M: Look, I'd like you to do what Kari did to see if we can get certain things straight about your feelings. Lie back flat again.

YAEL (*moving her head from Kari's lap*): If . . . if I could have a sheet, too?

M: To hide your face? Does it feel bad open?

YAEL: Yes, I guess so.

The sheet is put over her.

YAEL: I can't go to the sky. . . .

She becomes aware that someone's hand is brushing her face through the sheet and asks who it is.

KARI: It's me.

M: Who do you want?

YAEL: I want you.

M (*moving closer on the floor, touching her arm*): I would like you to take a trip to see your parents, and tell them what's happened to you since you've been ten.

YAEL (*her voice beginning to tremble softly with emotion*): It's, uh . . . very tough to do, because I feel, irrationally, that I didn't, uh . . . rescue them. Which I know I couldn't have.

M: First get in touch with them. If you like, you can tell them that, too. Do you want to go to the sky and talk to them?

YAEL: No, I can't go to the sky.

M: Into the sea?

YAEL: No.

M: Into a field? Into the earth? Where would their essence be, in smoke?

YAEL: Probably.

M: Smoke goes into the sky. Picture a very blue sky with a bunch of clouds about.

YAEL: Mmmmm . . .

M: Maybe some puffs of smoke will materialize into your parents. And when you see that, describe them.

YAEL: I have to separate them, because I know from when I was very small that they weren't happy together.

A street commotion is heard through the window. Bernard, Philip, and several others look out. Bernard reports that someone outside is being mugged. Yael remains lost in her own fantasy.

M (*to the others*): Hey, if you want to go to the park, go to the park. And if you're going to be here, be here. But shut up. (*To Yael:*) Do you want to talk to your parents separately? Are they fighting with each other now, or standing apart, or what?

YAEL: No, they're not fighting, but they're not very happy. . . .

M: Tell them everything that's happened to you since you've been ten, and what you feel about them.

YAEL: I can't do that.

M: Do it. Just start.

YAEL: I feel very little for my mother. I'd rather not start.

M: Do you see her? Do you have a picture of them both in your mind's eye?

YAEL: Yes.

M: Describe them.

YAEL: My father was very handsome. He had a moustache. . . .

M: Say, "My father *is* very handsome."

YAEL: My mother is, uh . . . rather ugly, and has a nervous twitch. For many years I hoped it wouldn't be hereditary. Uh . . . it must have been very difficult for them to live together. Maybe the answer to that is economic, in Germany at that time . . . Uh, I would tell them . . .

M: "I *am* telling them."

YAEL: I am telling them that I'm grateful that they sent me to Switzerland, because that was the way of keeping me alive.

M: What do they say when you tell them that?

YAEL: That they were happy to send me.

M: Now what do you want to tell them?

YAEL: Uh . . . that I'm not exactly living the way that they . . . the way that they brought me up.

M: Say, ". . . the way *you* brought me up." And what do they say to that?

YAEL: That the world has changed, and not to worry about it. That's what my father would be saying. No—both.

M: They speak as a Greek chorus?

YAEL: Uh . . . I think I was too small . . .

M: I thought you were going to say your father, and then you said both. How does it feel right now?

YAEL: Uh . . . I felt, uh . . . I felt I would scream at them. . . .

M: Then scream at them.

YAEL: Why didn't they—

M: Say it to them: "Why didn't *you*—"

YAEL: "Why didn't you leave Germany when you saw that things like that were coming? Why-why-why did you insist that things would get better? Because there was grandmother there? Why?" Why didn't they believe they should have left?

M (*as her alter ego*): "Why did you let me grow up as an orphan? Why didn't you come, too?" Now, what did they answer to that?

YAEL: That they just misjudged. That they thought it would pass by. And . . . uh . . . they were very loyal to Germany, they thought it would pass and that nothing would happen!

M: And what do *you* say about it?

YAEL: I also say something else: When I listen to some people complaining about their parents, I think that to an extent I was very lucky that I had none of these tremendous emotional problems of adolescents with parents, or of revolting, or of—

M: Can you tell them that? "I'm lucky I didn't have you when I was an adolescent."

YAEL: I don't know if I could tell them that.

M: Tell them, "I'm lucky I didn't have you." See what they do with that.

YAEL: They wouldn't understand it.

M: Tell them anyway.

YAEL: Well . . . "I'm lucky that I didn't have you when I was an adolescent, that I could do what I wanted to do, that I could take my own destiny in my hands from very, very young."

M: How do they feel about what you just told them?

YAEL: They would be sad.

M: Are they crying, both of them?

YAEL: Probably.

M: And how do *you* feel?

YAEL: I feel that it's probably useful. . . .

M: It's useful for them to be sad?

YAEL: Oh, no, no, no. It's useful for *me,* what I'm doing here.

M: They're sad. Now, how are you feeling?

YAEL: I feel I would tell them, "If you are alive, I would take good care of you, I would not push you around, or put you in an old age home. . . ."

M: How do they feel about that?

YAEL: Uh . . . they feel good.

M: How?

YAEL: Do you mean do they feel I make a sacrifice? I-I-I feel a tremendous sacrifice that they did by sending me away, their only daughter, and they're willing to let me separate from them. It must be terrible for them to separate, and not knowing what would happen. But they are willing to-to-to send me to safety! But it's a hard thing to live with. . . .

M: Tell them why it's hard.

YAEL: Because I feel that I should have done something to-to-to get them out!

M (*as her alter ego*): "I feel I shouldn't have resented you for not being around."

SARAH: Do you feel lonely?

YAEL: Um . . . sometimes. Right now, do you mean? Um . . . sometimes.

LITTLE PRINCE: No, did you feel lonely *then.*

YAEL: Yes. Very, very lonely. And I feel that I had a rotten deal, being in a very bad orphanage, um . . . being beaten up,

and in a bad place for six long years. But . . . uh . . . uh . . .
I feel that I became something from all that.

M: Do you want to tell them that?

YAEL: That the place was so rotten? They . . . uh . . . they
didn't have anything to do with that.

LITTLE PRINCE: Would you rather stay with them?

YAEL: Now?

LITTLE PRINCE: Then.

YAEL: I can't answer that, because I was too young. Uh, I
missed them badly. But when I could realize about the war,
and about the concentration camp, then . . . ah, I don't think
I wanted to be with them. I-I-I think that my instinct was
more . . . more to be living than to be with them.

M: Can you tell them that you hated them for leaving you
alone, and that you love them for giving you an opportunity
to live? See what they do with that.

YAEL: They were not sophisticated enough to be doing anything with that.

M: What do you want to tell them about yourself?

YAEL: I would tell them that I have two beautiful children, but
even so, I'm kind of mixed up a little. . . . (Her voice rises
to a quasi-laugh.) I'm managing. I have a lot of friends. I've
started in different countries to make a life for myself. On
the outside, I'm pleased with it.

M: And on the inside?

YAEL: On the inside, at times I have a tremendous . . . I have
a tremendous restlessness of the spirit, and I've always wanted
to learn more, and I've always wanted to do more, and I am
not satisfied with what I am. That's why I understand Bernard so much, this-this-this feeling about what do other
people think, for example. I don't talk about this because I
feel that people are just not interested. And I don't want to
burden them. Uh . . . I don't know if I would get more out

of life if I would tell more. I don't think so. But maybe . . .
uh . . . by asking.

M: Are there any things you want to ask your father?

YAEL: Ah, well . . . he married my mother when she was pregnant with me. If it were today, I would tell him, "Why did
you marry her if you didn't love her? There are other ways."

M: What does he say?

YAEL: He says, "Because . . . because she became pregnant, and
I can't give you the answers today, or the telephone number
for abortion."

M: You would have preferred to have him abort you?

YAEL: No. I'm pretty pleased to be alive. I would like to be
taller, or, uh . . . prettier, but I'm certainly pleased to be
alive. But I felt better when you were lifting me up there
than I am feeling down here.

M: Shall we lift you up again?

YAEL (*sitting up, pushing the sheet away, and opening her eyes*):
No.

M: What happened?

YAEL: I don't know.

M: Sure you do.

YAEL: Well, there's nothing specific in my mind.

M: You wondered when you started all this if you were going
to have the same kind of experience as Kari, but you felt
very good. Then you started to get uncomfortable. I was
wondering if you were touching on something that made
you feel the way she did.

YAEL: Well, I feel almost like crying, and I find it not so very
easy to cry. It's, uh, unusual for me to be crying.

M: So you keep a happy face?

YAEL: I keep a happy face for years. This morning everyone
said something about the smiling face, and it was very interesting to me that what I think I present, I really presented.

M: The feeling I get from you is, "I'm alive, and I should be appreciative about it. I'm alive, while my parents are dead. And I'm not supposed to resent anything or feel angry about my fate in any way. I should smile, even through the tears, otherwise I'm not an appreciative person."

SARAH: But you're both, aren't you?

YAEL: On the one hand, I'm fooling everybody by seeming always happy, and on the other hand I am *really* a happy person.

BERNARD (*curtly*): I don't think you're so hung-up.

YAEL: I'm sorry that I made you all so sad. I feel sorry about that.

BERNARD: My own reaction is that I'm sorry, extremely annoyed, that you're being put through all this. I think that while your feelings about all these things are perfectly normal and appropriate, it doesn't do you any good to have to talk about them in front of everyone. You're not the kind of person who enjoys telling everybody about the sore spots in your history.

JANE: Is it hurting her?

BERNARD: Yeah, I think she's less happy now than when we were picking her up.

ROBERT LEA: She may be less happy now because she thinks she made us all sad. You didn't make us all sad, Yael.

LITTLE PRINCE: That's right.

SARAH: Supposing we did get sad about your experience? Is that a bad thing? Do you feel everybody's got to be happy and laughing?

YAEL: You know, I always feel that . . . having to worry about other people.

SARAH: But feeling sad isn't such a bad thing. It can enrich our experience.

SHERSHONSKY: Do you feel you're worth less than anyone else here? Are you less of a person?

YAEL: I feel that I'm very small and ugly. Not enough people came into my life until later who said, "You're a nice person, nice to talk to, nice to look at." I feel that I have no right to make such a to-do about myself.

M (*playing her alter ego*): "I'm lucky to be alive. There's no sense in pampering myself beyond that point."

YAEL: Yes. But I get tears when I go to a railroad station, when I see people separating. No war. Just people kissing and separating. Then I get annoyed with myself for being so emotional, feeling sort of sorry for myself.

KARI: I look at a newsreel or a Thanksgiving parade, or the band marching, and it breaks me up.

ROBERT LEA: I love to cry. I go to a terrible movie, and I sit there with tears coming down my face. It's like a cathartic experience.

JANE: Yeah, for me too.

YAEL: I don't allow it to myself.

JANE (*shouting*): Why? Who will it hurt?

YAEL: I don't know. I have that from very small, from ten years old. For many years in that orphanage, people would say, "We're keeping you alive, you better be grateful."

JANE: And even though they beat you, and all that stuff, you're grateful to them?

YAEL: They kept me alive. I know what horrible people they were. But I am thinking that they had troubles, too. They were without men, and they were in a children's home. I should really hate them. . . . Uh . . . they used to tell us also that our parents were horrible to let us go. Especially one woman. She said that if she had children, she would never let them go. That was really . . . uh . . . terrible. That I carried with me all my life.

ROBERT LEA: You have children now. How would you have reacted in a similar circumstance?

M: So you couldn't hate the orphanage people for that, because you felt the same way about it. You also hated your parents for letting you go.

YAEL: They thought in six months it would be over and we would be reunited. . . .

M: I asked you to take this trip because there seemed to be a connection between your being rocked and this thing about your parents. I thought that if you could go back and talk to them, maybe the riddle would get unlocked. Now I have the feeling that all this talk is interesting historically, but that it isn't getting you in touch with anything else.

YAEL: I want to answer about my children: I don't think I would have the strength of saying I want to save them, and letting them go. I don't think so. . . . My daughter is now twelve and I'm having a hard time because she's three weeks away in Portugal on a vacation.

M: Also, I wanted to ask you—isn't it possible for you to hate some people at the same time that you're grateful? Does it have to be either/or?

YAEL: Yes, yes. I most of the time have to have things either/or.

M: In life it doesn't work out that way. It's often both. And I think you'd kind of give yourself a present if you could allow yourself to hate those orphanage ladies occasionally. And if you have mixed feelings about your parents, *have* them. Because you don't allow yourself to have both feelings, you've never felt free to criticize or hate.

ROBERT LEA: In a sense, your husband seems to have the same sense of duty and obligation towards you and your children that your father had with your mother.

M (*as Yael's alter ego*): "Yeah, and I can't allow myself to hate my husband in any way because I also love him and he's a nice guy."

BOB: You can do *both*.

SCENE 4: THE FIGHT

M: Listen, Bernard, I'd be interested in having you do something with Robert Lea. There's something going on between the two of you. There was, in the Lineup; and in a couple of other remarks you were making to him.

ROBERT LEA: Don't wrestle me, because I'm going to let you win right away.

M: Would you do it, Bernard, even if it won't show us anything about normalcy?

BERNARD: Uh . . . the only thing I'm good at is making love to girls. . . .

M: Okay, you don't have to make love to him. But I'd like you to do another nonverbal thing that might clear up some of the things you have going with guys like Robert Lea. Robert, take your glasses off, and then both men go to opposite corners of the room and look one another in the eye. Drop all preconceptions about each other. When you feel like it, start moving slowly toward one another, slowly. And when you meet, allow your bodies to do whatever they want to do.

> *The two men approach each other. Bernard bumps Robert Lea with his shoulder three times. The bumps are just hard enough to unbalance Lea slightly. Then, facing Lea, he puts his hands on his shoulders, and grabs them, making no further move. Lea responds by lunging at Bernard. Bernard responds by pulling Lea forward and flinging him over toward the couch. Lea misses the couch and strikes his head hard against the doorknob. For a moment he seems stunned, perhaps*

losing consciousness. Amid the shouting from the group, there are several female screams.

BERNARD: Oh, I'm sorry!

ROBERT LEA: Oh . . . shit!

The moment is a tense one. It would appear that Robert Lea has suffered a very severe blow.

PHILIP: I'm surprised you're still conscious!

ROBERT LEA: Oh, man! Am I bleeding?

KARI: No!

ROBERT LEA: Oooow! Wwwooow!

BERNARD: We ought to get a cold towel.

ROBERT LEA: Is it bleeding?

BERNARD: No.

ROBERT LEA: Ooohh! I'm surprised I'm still here!

BERNARD: I feel very guilty. . . .

PHILIP: I don't know what's the matter with you guys. I really don't!

ROBERT LEA: Do you have an ice cube, Marty?

M leaves the room and returns some minutes later with a towel full of ice.

KARI: I . . . That's why I've had it so good for these occasions. . . .

ROBERT LEA: That's why *what?*

KARI: Had it . . . you know . . . to make sense . . . or the outside . . .

She goes into one of her vague, abstracted moods while Bernard examines Lea's head.

BERNARD: It didn't break through the skin, but you're going to have a bump there. Put on some pressure, otherwise you'll get a real goose egg there.

ROBERT LEA (*holding the ice-towel against his head*): I'll tell you something—you really, really surprised me. And it's weird, because before, with Yael, when somebody was yelling for help outside the window, I really thought you wanted to help that guy, that you felt for him. And, now, how you can conceive of doing physical damage . . .

BERNARD: I didn't, I didn't! I wasn't trying to do it! I came up and I butted you because I wanted to get a feeling of how solid you were.

ROBERT LEA: I really presented a challenge to you. . . .

BERNARD: Didn't you notice? I didn't touch you first. I didn't try to wrestle with you.

Kari begins her mocking laughter.

ROBERT LEA: No. You were looking to smash me.

BERNARD: No! I wasn't! First of all, I don't, in all honesty, feel hostile to you.

ROBERT LEA: Oh, I can't believe that.

BERNARD: You don't threaten me. You haven't done anything to threaten me.

ROBERT LEA: I'm intellectually threatening to you.

BERNARD: No. Honestly, no. I would tell you if you did, but I felt no hostility towards you at all.

PHILIP: Was that *love?*

ROBERT LEA: Is it red?

BERNARD: Just keep the pressure on it.

YAEL: Leave it on a little while with the pressure on it.

Several people hover about Robert Lea, showing their concern, wanting to help.

PHILIP: Do you know how close to the temple that is?

ROBERT LEA: Yeah.

BERNARD: You had already told me you didn't want to wrestle with me. Besides that—I was a wrestler in college and I knew it wouldn't be fair to wrestle with you, and I didn't want to.

ROBERT LEA: Well, you certainly knew all the defense moves.

BERNARD: Yeah, but I did it to defend *myself.*

ROBERT LEA: Baloney.

BERNARD: This is the truth! Did nobody else . . . see?

ROBERT LEA: If you were a wrestler, obviously you knew the defenses.

SHERSHONSKY: And you shouldn't get involved in fighting.

ROBERT LEA: You used *offenses*. When I took hold of you, you wanted to take the offensive and show that you would be victorious.

M: He came at you to bump you, right?

ROBERT LEA: Right.

M: And he did it a few times and you stood there.

ROBERT LEA: Yeah, but the next time, I thought, he's going to give me a bump and I'm going to go flying over his head.

M: Right, right. But then instead of bumping you, he put his hands on you, and I thought it was kind of a bear hug, like a Russky embrace, and while he was hugging you you started to wrestle him. It came from you, not him, in spite of all your talk about closeness and niceness.

SHERSHONSKY: You did, Robert Lea. That was my reaction.

Bob agrees with Shershonsky and begins to reiterate what has already happened.

ROBERT LEA: I thought at the next bump I was going to go flying, so I thought I had to defend myself. You bumped me three times.

BERNARD: That wasn't necessarily aggressive. No one even talked about wrestling. I might have come over and kissed you, for all you knew!

ROBERT LEA: No, you would not do that, you would not do that. . . .

BERNARD: No, but I might have. I mean, you didn't know.

ROBERT LEA: You'd be incapable of that, actually.

M: Yeah, but he's saying the idea of wrestling came from you, that you were the first guy to bring it up, and that you were the guy who started wrestling.

ROBERT LEA (*chuckling*): Because he bumped me three times!

M: It doesn't matter.

ROBERT LEA: But the fourth time I could have been flat on my back!

BERNARD: No. I wasn't hitting you that hard.

ROBERT LEA (*touching his head*): How does it look?

M: It looks red. (*To Bernard:*) Do you think his bone is broken?

BERNARD: No. Just keep the ice on.

SHERSHONSKY: Why didn't you just let him bump you?

ROBERT LEA: Because I feel he has a thing with me.

PHILIP: What's this stuff about dropping preconceptions? I think it's impossible.

KARI: I do, too.

ROBERT LEA: I didn't have any preconceptions about him at all.

M: You did have a preconception he was going to wrestle with you.

ROBERT LEA: No. After he bumped me, man, this guy wanted to hurt me. He obviously knew I couldn't hurt *him*.

PHILIP: How did you know? You're just meeting him for the first time. How did you know?

ROBERT LEA: Because I know. I haven't raised a hand to anyone since I was in the service fifteen years ago.

BERNARD: Yeah, but you consider yourself the most aggressive person here.

ROBERT LEA: Intellectually.

BERNARD: We didn't say intellectually.

ROBERT LEA: I did.

KARI: There's nothing wrong with a good bump, right?

ROBERT LEA (*laughing*): On my head, there's something wrong with it.

M: Switch roles. Be him. Say what you think he thinks about you.

ROBERT LEA (*speaking as Bernard*): "You represent a challenge to me. I don't like you very much. You're an aggressive force to me. You've got your own big phallus, and you are attempting to castrate me."

M: Okay. Now Bernard, you be Robert Lea.

BERNARD: I'm not an actor. I can't speak in another person's voice.

ROBERT LEA: Do you want me to say what I think of you?

BERNARD: Yeah.

ROBERT LEA: I think you're not very sensitive. If you read a poem, or went to a play or a movie, you would walk out untouched by any of the art in it, or any of the emotions. You're really unable to empathize with another person ethereally. Physically is the only way you can get to another human, whether it's a woman or a man. You're much too analytic in the sense of being very clinical. You have what I would consider a CPA mentality.

BERNARD: You mean I don't have any real feeling for people?

ROBERT LEA: No. You don't. I think you're aware of that, and I think you really would like to have a feeling for people. I really like you, because I feel that you feel you were short-changed somewhere along the way, you were unable to acquire this esthetic concept of really communicating. Am I completely incorrect in my diagnosis?

BERNARD: Not completely. Uh . . . I'm much more sure of things I can see, and actually feel. This is true, but—

ROBERT LEA: You know why you had to ask all the girls here if they were turned on to you? Because you can't look someone in the eye and determine whether or not they like you, even for a moment. You don't read souls very well.

SARAH: You're really getting back at him now, aren't you?

ROBERT LEA: If it comes to a question of hurting him intellectually, I could do it.

SHERSHONSKY: You've *done* it.

ROBERT LEA: Like I could cut him up and rip him right down to the ground.

SARAH: Isn't that what you're doing?

ROBERT LEA: No. I'm being very gentle. My tongue can be much more cruel.

SARAH: Well, it sounds like that's what you're doing.

ROBERT LEA: Is that what I'm doing to you?

BERNARD: It seems to be what you're trying to do, but you're not succeeding because . . . uh . . . I don't feel defeated by it.

M: Because you're as insensitive as he says you are, so you don't feel it?

BERNARD: I . . . uh . . . just don't think he's hit home with any of these rapiers.

M: You feel he's being gentle?

BERNARD: I feel he would like to slice me up intellectually, but I don't think any of his points are accurate enough.

SARAH: If they aren't, then you're as insensitive as he says.

YAEL: I agree with Sarah.

JANE: He's saying that since what Robert says is wrong, it can't hurt him.

ROBERT LEA (*shouting*): Is any of this true?

BERNARD: That I'm insensitive to people, that I can't read souls?

ROBERT LEA: You can't read a poem and really screw the author as if the guy's really getting to you. If you go to a movie, you can't swing with Fellini or Antonioni.

BERNARD: That's the feeling I give you? That I can't do this?

M: Yes. You're an insensitive—

ROBERT LEA: Right. You're an insensitive person.

M: Otherwise, you're a nice guy.

BERNARD: Hhhmmnn. Right now, what am I supposed to say?

ROBERT LEA: Nothing at all.

M: How does that make you feel?

BERNARD: It doesn't hurt because I know he's wrong. Lookit. There are a lot of areas in which I'm very sensitive. I've exposed many of them tonight.

ROBERT LEA: You're most sensitive in a social situation. You have to make a good impression. That's the only thing that you've really demonstrated here tonight.

PHILIP: Doesn't everybody want social acceptance?

KARI (to Robert Lea): Are you the hippest person you know?

ROBERT LEA: One of the hippest. Yes.

KARI (derisively): Oh, I just love people who think they are the greatest!

SARAH: What really makes me mad is that you come on so self-righteous about it.

SHERSHONSKY: You're putting Bernard down, but the implication is that you can read the poem, you can see the movie.

KARI: That you can key in on Fellini.

ROBERT LEA: Right, right, right, right.

KARI: Oh, come on!

ROBERT LEA: But it's a statement of fact.

KARI: It's not a statement of fucking fact! Where's the fact?

ROBERT LEA: I demonstrate it constantly.

KARI: I would love to see you demonstrate it!

ROBERT LEA: All right, I'll do it.

> He picks a scene from Fellini's La Dolce Vita, and proceeds to analyze the symbolism with a good deal of brilliance.

KARI: Yeah, but you told me Fellini's feelings! Now let me hear yours!

ROBERT LEA: What . . . ?

KARI: How you keyed in to Fellini.

ROBERT LEA: Well, I have, uh . . . I have, for the duration of an esthetic work . . . I have an intellectual orgasm. I mean, it just gets my head turned on.

KARI: That's what I thought. It's the head that gets turned on.

ROBERT LEA: Well, when I have a relationship with a woman, I—

KARI: Don't I just love it, to have a man make love to me with his fucking head!

JANE: He's not talking about making love, he's talking about seeing movies!

ROBERT LEA: I . . . uh . . . do you want me to make love to you?

KARI: *No.* But you're trying to kick Bernard on a feeling basis, and, man, you know better. You're like two cock hens. . . .

BERNARD: Fighting cocks. That's the greatest image!

KARI: It incenses me. A man with violence . . . it incenses me. . . .

ROBERT LEA: It incenses me too.

KARI: Oh, yeah. You would have slugged him, instinctively.

ROBERT LEA (*to Bernard*): I only hope that you really didn't intend to hurt me. . . .

BERNARD: I told you I didn't intend to hurt you. Honestly, I didn't intend to hurt me, I mean—you.

ROBERT LEA: But you're not really sorry you did, are you?

BERNARD: I said I'm sorry. I don't like violence.

PHILIP: Why is it, then, that two nonviolent people come together with such violence? (*Laughter.*)

KARI: Marty can answer that. Let's hear about it, Marty. You're playing God here.

M (*to Kari*): I think you're nuts if you think I had a preconception of what they were going to do. I didn't expect them to do anything other than get something going where they could get into themselves and get a better appreciation of what they do to each other. And I was most struck that Robert Lea, in spite of all his talk of lovingness and whatnot, is the guy who started the wrestling. And I wonder if he'll think about that and see if it means anything to him or not. These procedures are designed to give people an opportunity to think things out about themselves, that's all.

JANE: Besides, Marty's not in control of them. Marty doesn't manipulate. They're adult human beings.

KARI: No, no, no. Marty has a certain responsibility in guidance of this thing.

PHILIP: Hey, Marty, there was something in the design of the situation which was inviting violence, it really was.

KARI: Yeah.

M: I did that because of some of the obvious hostile content I saw. I say, "Play this out"—and *they* thought they were going to kill each other. They stared like two gunmen at high noon for ten minutes and wound up grabbing each other. Unfortunately, we didn't stand around long enough, or well enough, to keep Robert Lea from getting his head banged, which I'm sorry for.

KARI: Yeah. I, too.

BERNARD: I think Marty really wanted to get in the opposite corner from me, but he didn't do it for some reason.

M: Wow! That's wild! You want to do that with me? Is that what you're saying?

YAEL: No more hitting!

M: It's like being on a horse.

JANE: You've got to get back on.

SARAH: Yeah.

BERNARD: No.

M: I didn't want to do it with you, but I'd be glad to if that's what's in your head.

BERNARD: Honestly, I don't want to, because it's going to be very violent, and I'll feel much worse, and I don't want to get back on that horse.

M: Let's do it in the other room, where there's less furniture. And we'll talk about it afterwards.

> *There is a great deal of commotion as M and the group move to the other room. All go, with the exception of Robert Lea, who is nursing his head. Yael tries to put a stop to the confrontation by begging them not to fight, but M asks her to stay out of it. There is an almost tangible presence of fear in the air, based on the group's belief that there will be great violence.*

Actually, the event turns out to be nonviolent, although there are signs that it might be, at certain points—particularly when M touches, or pulls, Bernard's beard. This gesture is made, in fact, to keep Bernard from talking away his feelings, but Bernard claims it is an aggressive act and threatens M not to do it again.

After some time of apelike approaches and retreats on the part of both men, they, and the others, return, unharmed, to M's office.

M: Do you want to sit down now and talk to me about it?

BERNARD: Yeah.

M: I'll tell you what was happening to me when I walked up to you. I didn't know what was going to happen, and I kept thinking that in one sense I'm not really prepared for this because my finger still bugs me. (*He is referring to a previous accident with a lawnmower in which part of his right index finger was amputated.*)

BERNARD: Yeah.

M: If someone twisted my finger, I think I would have hit the ceiling.

BERNARD: Yeah.

M: But I wasn't feeling at all, before, that I wanted a physical confrontation. I like you.

BERNARD: Yeah.

M: And when you said, "M wants to do it, but he doesn't have the guts to do it," or something, that was like really out of sight! Maybe you were telling me something that was in *you,* and I thought I'd like to do it with you because that last thing you had with Robert Lea must have really shaken the shit out of you.

BERNARD: I don't like it when people tweak my beard. It's a put-down I don't like.

M: I was just trying to shush your lips.

BERNARD: Oh.

SHERSHONSKY: I thought you wanted to fight.

BERNARD: Yes, I was looking for an excuse to . . . uh . . .

M: To punch me.

BERNARD: Yeah.

SHERSHONSKY: If he had gotten a little more aggressive and just shoved you once . . . oh, boy!

BERNARD: Yeah.

YAEL (to M): I didn't want to see any heads bashed. I-I-I could see him bashing your head.

M: I'm a big guy. I could take care of myself. You don't have to Red Cross me and save me and protect the world.

SARAH: She can try.

M: Yes, she can try.

BERNARD: Everybody likes a good fight, I think.

YAEL: No.

M (impatiently, to Bernard): Come on. What was going on between you and me?

BERNARD: The real feelings I felt, Marty, were that the hostility wasn't ever between me and Robert Lea. It was between you and me. . . .

M: Say "M," not real names.

BERNARD: You've ignored me periodically, as a form of putting me down, and I sort of felt that when I had the audacity to say that you wanted to get in a corner against me you probably would have liked to go through with it. If your finger was in shape. You would have liked to come out the top cock. And one of us would get his head smashed. And while I feel a certain exhilaration in a real . . . uh . . . a real combat, I felt that the price I would have to pay for this would not be worth it. I also had the feeling that most people wanted to see this go on.

SHERSHONSKY: What made you think everybody here wanted to see it?

BERNARD: I definitely had the feeling that the group wanted to see the fight, except—

YAEL: Except me!

ROBERT LEA: I didn't want to see it. I wasn't even in there.

SARAH: I didn't think there was going to be any fight.

YAEL: Why didn't you help me to stop them?

SARAH: I felt it would be very disrespectful to try to stop it.

BERNARD: Nobody helped stop it. Everybody says they didn't want to see the fight, but nobody—

There is now loud and overlapping protest from the group.

KARI (*trying to break through the noise*): I hate to see grown men fool around. Either you fight, or you don't. You don't play games.

SHERSHONSKY: M was kind of smiling and laughing, and he looked kind of silly. I think that you don't mind people being shitty to you, but it really gets to you when someone starts laughing.

BERNARD: That's exactly it.

SHERSHONSKY: I could see this boiling up in you.

BERNARD: Exactly.

BOB: My reaction is that at no point did M take the aggressive. What he did was either remain neutral, or attempt to provoke you by hitting on what he assumed to be your sensitive points. By making fun of you, or by touching you. You reacted. Oh, you had a ferocious reaction when he covered your mouth and told you not to talk! Almost compulsively, during those three or four minutes, you said, "Do you want to fight, do you want to fight?" M said nothing.

BERNARD: Everything you say is true.

SHERSHONSKY: When was the last fight you had?

BERNARD: Outside of college wrestling, I never had a fight that I recall.

SARAH: Even when you were a kid?

BERNARD: Yeah, but I don't remember when. It's been a long time.

JANE: Why didn't you hit M? He was teasing you, and you felt hostile toward him in the first place.

BERNARD: I'm not basically hostile toward him. I consider him my friend. You could be friends and have certain undercurrents of hostility.

JANE: Well, if you're friends and there's hostility, why can't you hit him?

BERNARD: I told you. If we started fighting it would really have been a bloody fight. I . . . I know Marty. He wouldn't go halfway. If we got going it would really be a wall-breaker.

PHILIP: You missed the beauty of what M was doing. He was acting like a primitive apeman, meeting another apeman.

SARAH: You know, he really did look a little bit like a gorilla.

YAEL: But I-I-I felt annoyed with you when you shut his mouth off. Why did you use that authoritarian gesture of shutting his mouth off?

M: Only because that was the rule. When people are not talking they often get more out of it.

BERNARD: Part of the difficulty between us today has been that I feel you haven't delineated your role. You've been coming in and out of things the whole time. Does anyone else feel this?

YAEL: I do!

KARI: I do too.

YAEL: But I feel there's no other choice. He must, to an extent, come in, and get out again. Come in and get out. I prefer that to having nobody have the thing in hand.

BERNARD: I think he should either be in or out. I don't know which is best.

JANE: Are you angry at Little Prince?

BERNARD: About what?

JANE: She hasn't been participating since early this afternoon.

BERNARD: Uh . . . I get the feeling she doesn't like what's going on. Every time she gets anxious she starts writing little notes to herself. (*Little Prince has indeed been writing things down for quite some time.*)

SARAH: I feel like Yael. I feel it's important to have somebody in charge, but also able to step out.

KARI: Yes, but it should be objective. There should be involvement, but a different kind. I felt today and tonight when he moves in and out like that, it does bother me.

M: Okay. So when it happens, talk about it.

BERNARD: I . . . I'd just like to say one last thing. I've criticized M for what I think is unfair staging of the rules, but I think also that some of the things he does do work. He's tried to construct a physical moment for everyone, just like the moment I had with Robert Lea, and I really felt something, a lot of feelings came out of that, whereas a lot of just plain talking, I felt, wasn't accomplishing anything. It's very hard, I think, to get a real physical process going among people who don't know each other, but some of these things work, and I think that's a good thing.

SCENE 5: SARAH'S LONELINESS

SARAH: I've already done my risk, but if nobody else minds, there's . . . there's something I'm distressed about for myself. I really haven't gotten very much involved in anything of my own. And it struck me that earlier I said there were several things distressing me, and one was loneliness. It struck me that maybe one thing about the loneliness I experience is that somehow I get into other people's things, but I don't get them involved in mine. (*She coughs.*) It struck me for about the last half hour that if I don't take some chance to try to do that, that I'll be leaving this group feeling that I haven't really done what I wanted to do for myself here. But I'm not sure how to go about it. . . .

BOB: Can you tell us some event, maybe?

SARAH (*after a contemplative pause*): I can't think of any event that would get me into it. I can get into something like the Indian wrestling with people. Somehow, physically I can get into something with somebody, and in a very safe way—because I know if I do something like that with a guy there's no chance of anything really happening. But that way I really feel involved and kind of exhilarated, and that's the only thing . . . (*Her voice trails off.*)

M: Suppose you just close your eyes and start to tell us what you feel like doing, and then let your body do whatever it wants to do. And if you get a notion that you want somebody to do something to you, or with you, tell us about it.

SARAH (*eyes closed*): Well . . . uh . . . one thing that I thought earlier was that I would really like to be rocked. Uh . . . that was one thing I thought of. . . .

> *The group lifts Sarah up and rocks her for three minutes, humming the syllable "*OM.*" Then they lower her to the floor, where she continues to lie.*

SARAH: I feel at peace . . . I feel relaxed, relaxed. And I feel good that so many people are touching me. . . .

M: What would you like right now? How would you like us to involve ourselves now?

SARAH: Well, I'd like to be asked something.

M: Who do you want to ask you something?

SARAH: You.

M: What could I do to make you feel stupendous?

SARAH: I'm not sure. . . .

M (*after a pause*): What could I do that would please you the most right now?

SARAH: You could hold my hand.

M takes Sarah's hand in his and holds it.

SARAH (*continuing*): What I'd really like to know from everybody is what it is they think I do that keeps them at such a distance, and leaves me in such a . . . (*Her voice trails off again.*)

KARI: A frailty. I feel a frailty. . . .

SARAH: You mean that I'd be hurt?

KARI: Yeah. Fall apart, maybe, so there might even be little pieces missing.

JANE: I feel a little helpless with you. Like your being strong, like your being self-contained . . . so that nobody has anything you'd want of them.

M: That's what I think too—so solid and beyond need that nobody has anything you'd want of them.

SHERSHONSKY: The same words went through my head. Self-contained. I had a feeling like, you know, that I would have nothing to give you, that you seem, well, you know, self-contained.

BERNARD: I feel a little different. I felt that you did want something from us. I, uh, didn't feel adequate to give it to you. Uh . . . I suppose that when I relate to women, I, uh . . . have to have more polarity. And I feel, relating to you, that I'm not sure I could, uh . . . not sure I would really be strong enough to give you what you wanted.

SARAH: You mean that I would want so much that you couldn't satisfy it? Or just that you wouldn't know what it is?

BERNARD: Um . . . you give the impression of an enormous amount of assurance, and, uh . . . I don't know . . . I'd feel very hesitant about asking you to go out into the other room and roll on the floor with me . . . um . . . whereas I can do it with some of the other girls here. And while I feel that you would probably like it, I feel that I would . . . um . . . not feel, uh, quite up to it with you because you might feel that I was, uh, a little bit ridiculous, and I couldn't quite put it over as I might with some of the others. . . .

SARAH: Hhhmmnn.

LITTLE PRINCE: I'd like to give you something, but, uh, I wouldn't know what to give you.

SARAH: As you can see, I'm not awfully good at saying what the hell it is I really want.

LITTLE PRINCE: That's what I thought.

M: Are you getting what you want now?

SARAH: Yes.

ROBERT LEA: That's not all you want. You want something more.

SARAH (*laughing*): I want what I'm getting, anyway, which makes me feel good.

M: Why don't you give her something she might want, Little Prince, even though she hasn't told you what, and then she'll tell you whether you're hot or cold, okay?

LITTLE PRINCE: Maybe you would like someone to come after you. . . .

SARAH: Yes . . . yes, I think I would. Yeah. I think you're very right. When I get wrapped up in my self-containment, I think I would like somebody to come after me.

BERNARD: Do you think we're all wrong in thinking that you're so self-contained and strong? Don't you feel that yourself?

SARAH: Oh, there's some truth to that. I know that's how I come on, and if so, that's part of the truth about me. But, um . . . it's certainly not all of it. I think the difficulty I have is in breaking out of that, in, you know, saying to somebody, *I want*, and *I need*.

LITTLE PRINCE: You did, and it came.

SARAH: That's right.

BOB: Is it possible for you to verbalize why you find it so difficult to ask for help?

SARAH: Well, um . . . one reason is, uh . . . in some part of me I kind of get it vicariously by being involved with others. But then, if you do that too much, it's very hard to get back on to yourself and be taken care of.

ROBERT LEA: What would happen if you asked and you got what you wanted?

SARAH: Well . . .

M: Like now.

SARAH (*loudly*): Right now, it's great. But I also feel a little embarrassed because of the feeling that maybe I shouldn't have asked, and—

LITTLE PRINCE: There's something wrong in getting it?

KARI: Or should it come without asking?

SARAH: It shouldn't—but that's certainly a grandiose fantasy I have, that it should come without my asking.

M: What we're doing now, is it going through a routine? Do you feel it's not sincere?

SARAH: No . . . I don't tend to feel that.

M (*resting his head on Sarah's chest and stomach*): Is my head too heavy?

SARAH: Uh-uh . . . uh-uh . . . no.

M: I'm having a great time.

SARAH (*laughing*): Well, that's good to know.

M: You've gone from a Number Two to a Number One. (*Laughter.*)

SARAH: What I was just thinking now was that if I didn't get so self-contained and come on so strong, I'd probably move from Number Two to Number One in lots of people's minds.

M: Yeah.

SARAH: And I think that's one of the things that keeps me lonely, and . . . and why I don't have a man in my life. I . . . uh . . . have a feeling of going to find one. I don't think I'm ugly. . . .

BERNARD: How do you relate to men when you're with them? Do you usually have satisfying relationships with them?

SARAH: Oh, I've had . . . Yes.

BERNARD: What goes wrong?

SARAH: Nothing, when I meet them, but not many of them come around. (*She and M laugh.*)

M: Seriously, then, I think a lot of them just don't know you want them around.

SARAH: Hhmmnn.

M: Men are kind of little boys, too. Like Bernard, they're afraid of being rebuffed. So you've got to go out of your way to tell him you're not going to rebuff him.

PHILIP: Smile at them.

M: Tell them they're needed sometimes.

BOB: Use your beautiful eyes.

Jane, Yael, and some of the others laugh warmly.

SARAH (*Sitting up and making a happy humming sound*): Great idea!

M (*after a pause*): Do you want to involve anybody else?

SARAH: No, not really. I've gotten almost everybody's feeling about it. I feel I've gotten some kind of answer, something I wanted to know, and that felt right. I felt like, uh . . . there was something mysteriously wrong with me, that I couldn't see . . . like a spot on the back of my dress, or a bad smell or something. . . .

M: Before moving on, I want to say that the whole Risk idea that we just did is that there are just an enormous amount of things people would like to do that they never get around to doing, from a sense that others will rebuff them, or turn them down. They think the rebuff is going to be so awful that they cut off the chance for a lot of satisfaction. The Hippies use the word "vibrations." People may not vibrate to you, but there's a better than even chance that if you respond to them they probably will. And I think that if each of us lived our lives more adventuresomely, we'd have a lot more payoffs in it. It's something to think about: how absurdly you limit yourself in some ways by not taking chances.

Act 7: Love Relationships

M: Now I'm going to ask you to try something else. I'd like you
to think of who in the room you'd like to have a love relationship with. And I mean that in the broadest sense—not necessarily just kissing or hugging. Maybe in terms of camaraderie,
affection, talking, staring, hand-holding. You define it. (*After
a pause.*) Is there anyone who hasn't thought of someone?

SHERSHONSKY: I haven't.

YAEL: I've decided that, right now, nobody.

M: Those of you who have, whenever you want to take your
turn, hold your hand up. When I call on you, walk over to
whoever you've chosen, without saying a word. You can then
see if your partner will nod his head for yes, or shake his head
for no. If you get a yes, you can proceed to have whatever kind
of relationship you want. If you want to have it in another
room, that's fine. Now . . . anybody want to start with Love
Relationships?

SARAH: Did you say a minute ago that we could talk to the
person?

M: Yeah. A love relationship would mean going outside and
having a conversation about how you feel: maternal love,
paternal love, filial love—whatever it means to you.

> *Considerable time elapses before anyone will make a
> commitment. Finally:*
>> *Sarah chooses Jane.*
>> *Philip chooses Little Prince.*

Bob chooses Shershonsky.

Bernard chooses Kari.

Robert Lea and Yael are left behind, unchoosing, and unchosen. Marjorie enters, for a rest period. M walks over to Robert Lea and plants a kiss on his head, at the place of his injury. M inquires about Robert Lea's wound and tells him that it doesn't look too bad.

There is more small talk for about seven or eight minutes, after which M rings a gong in his office to signal the others to return. He rings it several times without result.

ROBERT LEA: A J. Arthur Rank Motion Picture . . . !

There is another wait, another gong-ringing. Philip and Little Prince appear first.

PHILIP: Is that something you ring for patients when their hour is up?

The rest come back, with the exception of Bernard and Kari.

M: Listen, I was going to send out for pizza for dinner. There's a whole lot of other stuff out there, but if anybody wants pizza, let me know.

JANE: I do.

M: Does anybody else want any?

ROBERT LEA (*noticing Bernard's absence*): I'm not going out to get him. He's going to belt me again. That guy, he's a fucking idiot.

M (*amidst much laughter*): Who feels brave enough to go get Bernard? It's a woman's job.

JANE: I'll go, but if I'm not back in thirty seconds . . .

M: Anybody else want some pie?

SARAH: I'm not hungry now, but I think I will be later. How late can we order?

M: Up to midnight.

PHILIP: You know someone who can get pot?

SARAH (*joking*): Yeah, call out and order some pot.

BOB: The day will come.

M (*to Philip*): Your Risk passed a long time ago. No pot.

Jane returns with Bernard and Kari.

M: Now let's go into what it was like: the people who went out —and the people who stayed; what transpired, how you felt.

BOB: I was really glad to go out with Shershonsky. I mean, I've been sort of thinking about it for some time now. Uh, I sort of felt we had a close affinity in terms of hang-ups, backgrounds, hang-ups, experiences, hang-ups . . . and I wanted . . . uh . . . to talk to him about some of his thoughts, and I think we had a very good exchange. Do you want to know what we talked about?

M: Sure.

BOB: I told him I felt we had a great number of things in common, for example his difficulty in saying to people, "I love you," and his reticence or reluctance to kiss people, and his reluctance to compete. I think I could learn a great deal from him in terms of what he's done so far in opening himself up in relationships with others.

SHERSHONSKY: Well, uh, I was a little surprised that Bob asked me to go out, and we started talking, and like getting through, and it was like . . . like a nice thing. I saw some things in him, like during the day, that sort of bothered me, except like I've always been a slow starter in everything I've ever done, and I have the feeling sometimes I'm like ten or fifteen years behind, and he seemed sort of younger in a way, and it's like great that he's kind of wigging things out for himself instead of, you know, drifting along, which is sort of what I've done. It was just kind of nice talking to him.

BERNARD: I think it's nice that you two guys went out together, because I felt the whole day that you two have a great deal in common. You're the two most alike people here, in a sense. You're the two nicest people here, I think. Uh, the sweetest people here.

KARI (*suddenly shrieking*): You're cringing! I knew it, I knew it, I knew it!

M: Shershonsky cringed?

KARI: Yeah, he cringed.

BERNARD: I've often wondered how people like this react to each other. Very often they're put off a little bit by each other because they might not like these qualities completely. But, um, I'm glad that you two guys seemed to like each other. . . . I, uh, think it's a nice thing.

SHERSHONSKY: I, uh, have a very good feeling about Bob. But this thing about my being a nice guy, when someone says that, it disturbs me, it really bugs me. A nice guy . . . I don't know what that means.

ROBERT LEA: Nice guys finish last.

SHERSHONSKY: What bugs me is that I know I'm not that totally nice a guy. I like to try not to come on strong, and I try not to bug people too much, but also, like, you know, there's anger down there. I've been in scenes where I wasn't a nice guy.

ROBERT LEA: But you felt guilty about it later on.

SHERSHONSKY: Yeah, I felt lousy about it.

ROBERT LEA (*with an understanding laugh*): Well, that means then that you're a very gentle, sweet person, and this I find very admirable. I mean, I wish people would say that about *me*.

BERNARD: It's funny about how me and Robert Lea both react the same way to you guys, 'cause *we're* so much alike. We're both a couple of pricks when you get right down to it, and—

M: Except he's the sensitive one. (*Laughter.*)

BERNARD: That's right.

YAEL: But he's not anymore.

BERNARD: Anyway, I think that we both share, uh, sort of an admiration . . . I certainly do. I shouldn't speak for—

ROBERT LEA: I do too.

BERNARD: I just have a tremendous admiration for people who are lucky enough to be born like that.

ROBERT LEA (*to Shershonsky*): But the thing is, I'm really like you basically, and this whole other type thing is a façade. It is fear, because you're going to get hurt. I could be bugged. Like a little girl on the elevator did something the other day, and I opened my mouth, and I felt just terrible because she was just a lovely, lovely girl, and I probably hurt her, and it just bugged me terribly.

SHERSHONSKY: Well, I feel very funny when you say these things about me, because it projects me into a situation which makes me uncomfortable. Like people expect me to be a certain way, and I have to, you know, live up to a certain image. I'd rather be off here on the side.

ROBERT LEA: Well, my role is I play another part. Actually, I like to live very square, and be very square, and—

SARAH: But you're really very hip.

ROBERT LEA: But I like to blend into the atmosphere.

SARAH (*to Shershonsky*): You know, I didn't have that "nice guy" feeling about you.

KARI: No, me either.

SARAH: I felt you were the most attractive man in the group, and I really wanted to get something going with you, and I tried several times, and you seemed so standoffish that then I got kind of put off by that.

SHERSHONSKY: That's funny, because I really liked that contact with you, uh, you know, the wrestling thing.

SARAH: Yeah. . . .

M: That's doubly funny, because when you had a chance to pick someone you didn't raise your hand to pick him, and he was available in the beginning, which is the whole thing you went through on the floor, with your loneliness thing.

SARAH: Right . . . right.

SHERSHONSKY: And that's extra funny because if you hadn't gone
off with Jane, I would have liked to have taken you out.

SARAH: I thought of picking you, and then I felt put off, or, you
know, that you wouldn't want it or something. Then I had
also wanted to pick Jane. I hadn't had any chance, really, to
have anything going with her at all.

JANE: Oh, I'm second-best, huh?

SARAH (*amid some laughter*): No. You were both on my mind.

BERNARD: I think that's very important, Sarah. I think what's
really operating here is that you were afraid of being rebuffed
by someone. It's a good example of how you wouldn't have
been rejected although you thought you might be. This might
be an interesting insight.

YAEL: I wanted Shershonsky to pick me, but I said to myself,
"Well, let's see what happens if I don't take the initiative."
And what happens is that I was sitting here without anybody.

M: How do you feel about that?

YAEL: On the one hand, I was a little bit glad because I was a
little tired. On the other hand, I felt that I should talk to
Robert Lea in here because I felt sorry for him, with the
head, and I was glad that he was laying down and, uh, communicating—that he was happy too at not having to make
conversation. And then I felt when M kissed him, or what
you call kissing, that M should have come over here and
kissed me too, but I didn't say anything. I hesitated to play
Red Cross, but when I don't play Red Cross, then I'm being
left over.

M: A nurse is someone who's always patching up other people,
protecting other people, self-sacrificing. That's a Red Cross
job.

JANE: It's not Red Cross when you ask for something for yourself.

YAEL: But I didn't really feel strong when you asked, "Does anybody feel strong about anybody?" I just felt very tired, physi-

cally, and mentally tired, and not enough to put into anybody. *The group is indeed beginning to show signs of fatigue. Sarah, especially, has begun to look slightly wan, to close her eyes for brief periods, and she is now trying to stretch out on the floor, leaning on her elbow. A number of sandwiches have been made and eaten during the almost twelve hours of the marathon's span thus far; a good many sodas and paper cups full of coffee have been consumed. But there has been no set, or substantial, meal. With fatigue, however, tension has been abating: The rather steady parade of bathroom-going has lessened considerably within the past several hours.*

M: How about the rest of you who were out?

JANE: I was very glad when Sarah picked me, because I don't really know very many women. I have two girlfriends, and I'd like to have more relationships with women, and I'd like to feel more secure about relating to women. I mean there was a whole period in my life where I hated all women and I didn't want to have anything to do with them. And I find it impossible to relate to them except as a threat, or a mother, or as a competitor, or something like that.

YAEL: That's very interesting, because I liked very much your hand on my head, and I saw that you had your hand on Sarah's head, too, so there must be some feeling.

JANE: Yeah. Yeah, it's something I would like to have. And the other thing that I really like about this is people don't touch each other, but there's been a lot of physical things going on in the room, and it's really beautiful.

M: Do you want to tell us what you talked about, or did, or felt, or got out of it?

SARAH: Well, our questions didn't go very far because of the taboo on asking people what they do, but I had good vibrations about Jane in the beginning. I really admired her forthrightness, and also some of the things which she had seemed to work out for herself about men, and sex. And I also admired some of the interventions she made in various things that were going on in the group which I thought were very effective. We just tried to get to know each other. We both realized that we're really reserved people. If we really wanted to get to know each other, it would take a lot longer time than just five minutes.

Jane laughs and concurs with what Sarah has said.

M (*after a pause*): How about the rest of you?

BERNARD: Well, I asked Kari to go out with me because she's been turning me on increasingly all day, been, uh, progressing geometrically. So I felt the need to evoke some response, preferably a physical response, or some sort of emotional response. We went out and we talked and I felt, uh, part of the hostility had disappeared. But I felt there was still a reluctance on her part to have a physical relationship, and so I made no attempt to, although I wanted to. I felt that she was very confused about this, and so I didn't try to make an advance.

Robert Lea guffaws softly.

BERNARD (*continuing*): So we talked, and I enjoyed the brief interlude we had. I felt there was something going on between us that hadn't before. Before there was nothing going on between us except for some, uh, slightly erotic fantasies of my own.

KARI: In a group, I do behave different. I had reactions to Bernard, feeling he's obnoxious, and all that. I'm obnoxious sometimes. I don't think there should be anything wrong with being that at times. And I tried, at least, to get that feeling across—plus except once I was not honest in doing something I should have done. Once I really felt like touching him, and I didn't react to it.

M: To touching Bernard?

KARI: Yeah, I didn't, at the time. . . .

She goes on disjointedly, attempting to explain that she is not clear about her own "physical thing."

M: What do you feel about Bernard physically?

KARI: He doesn't turn me on physically. You know. I don't want to have, uh, physical intercourse with him. I don't think it would even turn out pleasant.

M: Physical intercourse? You mean holding or touching?

KARI: Fucking.

M: But you said you wanted to touch him. That's physical intercourse.

KARI: No, no, it was just touching. But when I say *intercourse,* I mean *fucking.*

M: Oh. But you'd like to touch him?

KARI: No. Only one time during our thing together. I felt he was being hurt, and, oh, I felt like going over and just shaking his head.

M: Gee, with this prohibition about touching that you talked about, it's conceivable to me that you think you either have to sit on a chair and not having anything to do with someone, or you have to fuck him. There's a big gamut, you know, between fucking and sitting on a chair.

Kari tries again to organize her verbalizations, but with little success. There is, however, some sense of her not wanting to hurt Bernard.

M (*to Bernard*): You ought to observe yourself in places where you stop short. You might have been right if you had touched her. She might have objected, but then again maybe she wouldn't have.

BERNARD: No, I was probably right. If I had made an overture, I probably would have been rejected, and, uh, come out feeling miserable.

M: Maybe not. You could have looked at your vote again.

JANE: If you're rejected, why do you necessarily come out feeling miserable?

M: Look at the voting slips, Bernard!

ROBERT LEA: Just think! After you get rejected twice, you can get eight acceptances.

BERNARD: That's obviously my problem: Eight acceptances don't make up for *one* rejection.

KARI: How would it be to be accepted as a human being, not as a lover? Do you have to be accepted as a great lover?

BERNARD: Mmmnn . . . yes.

KARI: Why?

BERNARD: Why not? Why *not?*

KARI: That's fine, but when there's no possibility, couldn't you be accepted in any other position?

PHILIP (*to Bernard*): What kind of relationships do you have with men?

ROBERT LEA: Do you punch?

BERNARD: Physical, physical.

M: It's okay as long as they don't touch his beard. (*Laughter.*)

BERNARD: With men I have physical relationships, strangely. . . .

PHILIP: What do you mean by that?

> *Bernard explains that his relationships with men consist of playing tennis, skiing, and other forms of physical competition; also that he finds nonsexual relationships with women boring.*

M: You just said that you got pleasure out of talking to Kari, though.

BERNARD: Maybe I exaggerated. I found her not quite as tough a broad as I thought she was, but still a little distant.

SARAH: So with men you fight, and with women—you screw.

BERNARD: Right. Exactly.

LITTLE PRINCE: Bernard, what if you're impotent?

BERNARD: What if I were—??? But if I were, then I'd be a different person. I mean, what can a guy say? I'm not.

LITTLE PRINCE: But I mean . . . to accept the possibility of it. You're only stipulating women-relationships as purely sexual.

Bernard says that he has platonic relationships with women who are married to his friends, but repeats that his major pleasure lies in "treating women as women"— that is, sexually.

JANE: You mean "holes," right?

KARI: Holes!

JANE: That makes me think about what Robert Lea was saying about you. . . .

BERNARD: That I'm insensitive?

JANE: That you're insensitive, and the only way you're worth anything is if you can give somebody a good lay.

PHILIP: Seriously, you know, you can't live like that.

Jane and Bernard continue to argue the point, but Bernard sticks rather staunchly to the truth: Women, for him, are basically sexual objects. He adds that he does not consider himself a neurotic individual, and that he feels no need for psychotherapy.

M: Okay. How about Philip and Little Prince?

LITTLE PRINCE: I feel very, very good. I felt absolutely awful, awful, awful since I came back from the park, and I was hoping Philip would talk to me. He's the person I associated most with in the room and wanted to get to know. Not just in a physical way, but in all ways. In immensity. I didn't really understand why M did to me what he did to me before. It was awful, and I was rather down, I felt utterly hopeless for those few hours. But now I feel good about myself again.

JANE: How did that happen?

LITTLE PRINCE: It doesn't take much, and that's what's frightening. It bounces back from one direction to the other direction. But I feel calm now.

BERNARD: You feel loved. That must have given you a lot of belief in yourself once again.

ROBERT LEA: What did Philip say that made you change?

PHILIP: We didn't *say* that much. There was a tremendous attraction between us. I could almost see force lines emanating between us.

ROBERT LEA: But you saw it in here, too.

PHILIP (*looking at Little Prince, who giggles and blushes*): Yeah. And I really feel good because I feel that we have a chance to, uh, really help each other in lots of ways.

BERNARD: Why do you need help?

PHILIP: Well, I need help in my relationships with other people.

M: You're one of the few people I don't know anything about on the basis of anything that's happened here.

PHILIP: Well, specifically, I have a problem. . . . I have a girl-friend, and I would like to sleep with other girls, know them intimately, and, uh, I don't think my girl does. She doesn't want to know other guys. I want her to, but at the same time I would want her not to. It's selfish, I guess. . . .

ROBERT LEA: You were brought up on that your whole life. You're just hung up on a ritual, that's all. Man is trying to break out of his whole fucking . . . rituals.

M: What do you mean, rituals?

ROBERT LEA: The rituals of the Ten Commandments, the rituals of loving thy neighbor, and do not covet someone else's wife. Still, men go around and fuck other girls and sow their oats, but women don't do that. It's all right for Dad to do that, but not for Mommy, 'cause Mommy *never* got laid. Mommy just like had an Immaculate Conception, and there you were! And you're trying to break out of this box, this concept of doing Wrong, Wrong with a capital R.

LITTLE PRINCE: I think the reason we felt the ties is because I'm going through the same thing with my lover. But we've come a long way to the point where we're both relaxed enough with the idea that other relationships will enhance our rela-tionship. All I can say is, now we have to go out and experi-ence it as being true.

ROBERT LEA: You like that part of yourself, though? The part that carries on?

LITTLE PRINCE: What do you mean, carries on?

ROBERT LEA: The histrionics.

LITTLE PRINCE: You mean the theatrics of everything I do?

ROBERT LEA: Well, histrionics.

LITTLE PRINCE: Yeah. When it's theatrics, it's like *real*. If I'm not standing on a window ledge threatening to jump out, it doesn't seem real, somehow. If I'm not smashing glasses against a wall, or pouring tea over Art, it doesn't seem real. But that's also a cop-out where it's so real I can't stand it anymore. But I've got to learn to stand it.

> *Shershonsky says, at length, that Little Prince's changes of mood and personality strike him as rather frightening, that the pattern of her highs and lows is "a kind of scary thing."*

LITTLE PRINCE: I feel that, too. It's frightening because I know me in my rational state, and when I'm irrational I can remember the rational me, but she seems out of reach. Forgive me for quoting, but—

M: I won't forgive you.

LITTLE PRINCE: You won't, for quoting?

M: No, I won't forgive it.

LITTLE PRINCE: All right, you won't forgive it.

M: No. I won't.

LITTLE PRINCE: Okay.

M: I don't understand the whole quoting business with you.

LITTLE PRINCE: Well, it's just part of me.

JANE: Say it in your own words.

LITTLE PRINCE (*loudly, defensively*): Okay! I'll say it in my own words although I'd like to quote!

M: You don't have to quote them, but you can say it in their words.

LITTLE PRINCE: I just don't like taking other people's words and using them. I have this hang-up about literature. . . .

M (*playfully*): Everybody takes from somebody else. There isn't a thought anybody has in this room that's original. My mother once said so forth and so on, and this thought I got from Marjorie, and the next thought I got from Ronnie. You can go on endlessly. So you say, "T. S. Eliot said it." You're going to have a clean record. Ahead of time you're going to say, "As T. S. Eliot said . . . ," and you're protecting yourself, and that's crazy.

LITTLE PRINCE: It's because I dig T. S. Eliot and I dig what he says!

ROBERT LEA: What did he say?

LITTLE PRINCE (*somewhat jokingly*): Oh, whatever he said!

M: You said before you want to cut down on the amount of things you say. You can cut five percent out of the words you use if you don't attribute everything to its source.

LITTLE PRINCE: Okay, just let me say one sentence: "We're at the same time what we cease to be, and what we're going to be, and during that time you've just got to do the best you can."

YAEL (*laughing*): Now I want to know who said that!

LITTLE PRINCE: I'll tell you after.

KARI: Philip, may I ask you a question? Do you ever take LSD?

PHILIP: Once.

KARI (*to Little Prince*): Did you?

LITTLE PRINCE: I wanted to tomorrow, but I don't think so—after today.

BERNARD: I highly suggest that you don't. That's my opinion.

M: Kari, why did you ask Philip that question? Do you want to tell him something about himself?

KARI: Oh, no. I still have the same feeling that I had when I first met him. Pretentious, and . . . still tied up in knots.

PHILIP: How do you mean?

KARI: Well, you can't express yourself.

PHILIP: My stomach was tied up in knots when you first said it.

KARI: You haven't been personal all night, all day. When you first came in, and Little Prince, everybody looked up, and boy! Hippie-Yippie, we're going to see how they really live, and . . .

M: "I'm Kari, and I'm trying to say to you, Philip and Little Prince, that I thought you had the problem licked, and you'd be into sexual freedom, and—"

KARI (*shrieking with laughter*): Yes! That's it!

M (*continuing as her alter ego*): "—and you'd be loose! But you came back into the room together and you don't have anything to say other than you had a nice talk, and—"

> *Philip and Little Prince begin to laugh.*

M: "—and she says, 'He made me feel reassured because he liked me'—and he says, 'I'm hung up with my girlfriend, and I have a problem'—and she says, 'I'm hung up with my boyfriend' "—

> *The group is now howling with laughter, but laughing loudest are Little Prince, Philip, and Kari.*

M: Right?

KARI: Right! Right!

M: And you thought they'd be great, but you're not envious anymore.

KARI: No, I'm certainly not! (*To Philip:*) Not that I really thought of you for a moment as a Hippie, I really didn't, but if you dress in those clothes . . . well, there's a role-playing there that I don't have. I don't take on a role and I don't get into a costume unless I feel really comfortable.

LITTLE PRINCE: I really feel comfortable. . . .

KARI: No. I sense from you at times that you don't feel comfortable about it.

LITTLE PRINCE: How can I . . . how can I change?

KARI: I don't know how.

LITTLE PRINCE: How can I change twenty-one years of conditioning in a year . . . ?

KARI: I don't know, I don't know.

LITTLE PRINCE: I've changed so many things in six months . . . I've—

KARI (*shouting*): I don't know! I don't know! I have inhibitions about *myself* physically, right?

LITTLE PRINCE: Yeah.

BERNARD: What kind of inhibitions?

KARI: Well, uh, I can't dress up like she does. It makes me very, uh . . .

BERNARD: Why not?

KARI: No. It would make me self-conscious. I can do it at home, or with one guy, or with my husband, but I can't do it in a public scene. I like to have a relationship with my body that is me and my own. I don't think I could ever get beyond that.

LITTLE PRINCE: I get hung up on it, too. Like many times you see me trying to pull at this bra thing, all night long, right? But you have to discipline yourself not to get hung up, because, after all, it's nothing. What is it?

Act 8: Nudity

SCENE 1: UNDRESSING

M: This is a point where we can move on to something else. I want to get into some of the other ways in which people are hung up. What I'm going to do now is undress, and I want everybody else to undress also.

KARI (*with a sigh of real despair*): Oh, shoot . . .

LITTLE PRINCE: Completely undressed?

M: Completely.

KARI: Oh shoot, oh shoot . . . Okay, Marty . . . it had to be! Oh shoot . . .

> *Kari continues to heave and sigh as the others begin to undress. Someone jokes about preferring to undress in the bathroom, but by and large the act of disrobing is performed in silence, except for the muted wails of Kari. Jane takes her name tag from her clothes and places it over one breast, which evokes a good deal of laughter. Initially, all undress with the exception of Kari, Yael, and Sarah.*
>
> *The mounting fatigue of the past several hours disappears within seconds and is replaced by tense alertness.*
>
> *M, the first to finish disrobing completely, sits down, draws one leg up to his chair, and sprawls in an attitude*

of ease. Yet, he is surrounded by a good deal of self-consciousness and nervous giggling.

M: Throw your clothes under furniture to keep them out of the way. Then stand up and walk around the room and shake hands if you like. You're all grown-up people.

LITTLE PRINCE (*to Philip, breathily*): You're beautiful! You really are!

They laugh together, uneasily, as Philip, tall, slim, and extremely boyish, blushes and seems to hang his head in embarrassment.

BOB: With those clothes you had on, off—it doesn't really make much difference! (*More laughter.*)

M: Does anyone want to touch, other than shaking hands?

There is now further touching: hands on shoulders, chests, arms, hips; but all gestures are made timidly and with much self-awareness. Only M, making the rounds from one person to the next, seems to be enjoying himself. As a final gesture of friendliness, he shakes hands with Bernard's penis.

BERNARD (*to M about Kari*): You ought to make her undress.

KARI: You can't make me.

M: I can't make anyone do anything they don't want to do.

PHILIP (*to M*): Tell me . . . are you at *all* uncomfortable? You look a little . . . uh . . .

M: No. I feel exhilarated.

KARI: M is not uncomfortable. This is what he's been waiting for all night!

PHILIP: Everybody looks good. . . . Everybody looks a lot better. . . .

LITTLE PRINCE: Yeah (*Laughter.*)

SARAH (*clothed*): I feel like a voyeur.

YAEL: I don't feel like a voyeur. I feel envious that they can do it so fast, and I have to say to myself, "Oh, I'll wait a little while and maybe the time will come. . . ." I don't feel like a voyeur.

BERNARD: Kari, I'm sorry I said I think M should make you do it. I can understand why you might not want to, but could *you* at least tell us why you don't want to?

Kari makes no reply.

M: Why don't the three clothed women sit in the center and talk about what it feels like to be fully clothed in a room full of naked people.

SARAH (*settling to the floor*): Sure.

YAEL: Oh boy, am I glad I'm not the only one!

KARI (*sitting down beside Sarah and Yael*): It's old hat with Marty.

SARAH: It's almost as bad as being the only naked woman in a room of clothed people.

KARI: It sure is, it sure is.

As the rest stand about nude, M embraces Little Prince and lifts her off the floor for a moment.

ROBERT LEA: You dirty old man! (*Laughter.*)

BERNARD: Marty, you're the only guy I know who is more lecherous than I am. (*More laughter.*)

ROBERT LEA: Etymologically, lecher means *to lick.* (*Still more laughter.*)

BERNARD: Is that right?

ROBERT LEA: Isn't that right, Yael? From the Germanic *lechen?*

YAEL: *Lechen.* Yes.

M (*to the three clothed women*): You gals carry the ball, will you?

PHILIP: To what?

KARI: To where?

PHILIP: That's funny, too.

M: Talk among yourselves. Tell how you feel.

SARAH: As I said, I feel a bit like a voyeur, but I don't want to take my clothes off.

KARI: Why don't you?

SARAH: I don't know why. I just don't want to. And if I did, I would be doing it just because everybody else is doing it. But I don't think I should just go along with the crowd.

YAEL: And that's that.

M: But if you did know, then why?

SARAH: Well . . . oh, damn it! You know, this is one thing I don't think is particularly a hang-up. I think it would be more of a hang-up on my part if I *were* to undress now. I really don't feel I want to. I wouldn't be comfortable about it.

M (*persisting*): But if you *did* know why you didn't want to?

SARAH: Well . . . I know some reasons. . . .

M: What are they?

SARAH: One reason I don't feel too good about displaying my body is because my breasts are saggy, and I've got a scar on my middle from a Caesarean. And, you know, lots of things . . . (*She trails off.*)

BERNARD: But you also thought Shershonsky wouldn't go out of the room with you. Maybe you're wrong. Maybe we'd like your body.

SARAH: That's true, you might. But I'm not sure that I really want to expose it.

SHERSHONSKY: You're not sure that *you'll* like it?

SARAH: Uh . . . that's right.

SHERSHONSKY: You're not sure that you like it yourself, maybe.

SARAH: I used to like my body a lot. I still do. I don't dislike my body.

SHERSHONSKY: Do you like yourself? Do you like to be with yourself?

SARAH: Yes. I think I like myself. I'm getting used to . . .

YAEL (*after a pause*): I have probably some of the same reasons. I don't know. I have two things. I have been in a situation like this. I have been swimming nude in a lake very frequently, and enjoyed it with friends. Uh . . . I have been in a nudist sauna, and I didn't get especially aroused with the men and women naked. But I feel here very surprised that uh . . . Shershonsky did undress, because the way he was sitting, I said to myself, "Ah, at least one man we will have who won't undress." Another reason that is not necessarily oppressive: that is the Caesarean sections which didn't do my body so good. The other, the more serious reason is that if I would undress and try to find a man to either hold hands or hold me in his arms, I would not just . . . I-I-I wouldn't be satisfied with that. I would want . . . I would want more. So instead of getting myself into a situation . . . uh . . .

JANE: A situation like Jane is in!

YAEL (*laughing*): She has a wonderful sense of humor. . . . Well, instead of getting myself into a situation where I would feel more frustrated, I-I-I wanted . . . I-I-I hoped M would overlook me, and nobody would pay any attention. But . . . but I didn't feel upset by seeing everybody else.

SARAH: No, I don't either, but—

YAEL: Especially I think that Jane has a beautiful body, and, uh, I enjoy it—a good body of a woman. But I-I-I feel it's so artificial that it would put me in-in-in a situation of getting very aroused and then having to walk out.

SARAH: Yeah, I have some of that going on too. I really would probably feel like screwing with somebody if I got naked and close to somebody physically.

BERNARD: So why don't you, why don't you?

JANE (*to Yael*): Did that happen when you went swimming?

YAEL: Well, I went swimming with friends. . . .

M: I don't know about the chicks, but a prick-count shows me that nobody's got an erection.

YAEL: That's a very bad reflection about *us*.

M: I'm just saying that of the male members, you can tell nobody looks like they feel like screwing.

SARAH: That's even worse.

YAEL: Yeah, that's even worse!

Kari cackles loudly.

There is some indication on the floor that Philip may *have an erection.*

M: Philip, you've just got a big prick. (*Laughter.*) I don't imagine your big brother is bigger than you in member. Is he?

PHILIP: Uh . . . I've got him there. We've never really measured, but—

YAEL (*continuing with Jane*): The swimming situation was the ideal setup because we went with friends, and then I could go to bed with . . . uh . . . um . . . my husband, and think maybe about the guys in the water. Uh . . . with them I would either touch, or lie on an air mattress or something like that, but—

BERNARD: You're cheating your husband.

YAEL: Mentally, yes. I have said that before. In fantasy.

JANE: I just find it hard to believe that you feel that if you take off your clothes you're automatically going to be aroused.

BERNARD (*to Yael*): What makes you different from these other girls?

JANE: I mean, you're *looking* at everyone, and you're not aroused, so how—

M: You had all those feelings in you about blocking in, and keeping out, and why don't you turn on, and you don't have orgasms. So why don't you take a chance and undress and see what happens? You can join us. You can change your mind. You're allowed to.

YAEL: I can dress again? Is that all right? You see . . . that's what happens . . . that's the group pressure. Because I feel that now, on the one hand, I would like to; and on the other hand, I wouldn't like to. I feel that the group really pressures me. . . .

M: Do it if it feels right for you.

BERNARD: I'm not pressuring you.

JANE: I don't think you should peel if you don't feel like it. I'm just asking you *why*. I don't think it's the reasons you've given.

M: And I'm telling you there might be some connection with the thing you were wrestling with before. I mean, life is a series of putting on and taking off your clothes, in a sense. You ask if we'll let you put them on again. You'll have to put them on, and it will be your choice when you want to. We're not going to send you out into the street naked. (*Laughter.*)

YAEL: All right, if I can sit next to Shershonsky. I'll take them off!

> She rises from the circle and begins to disrobe to the accompaniment of cheers and applause.

YAEL: Oh, I forgot! Turn that tape off!

M: Why?

JANE: Do you think they can *hear* your nakedness?

M (*turning back to Kari*): Ah, what's with *you?*

KARI (*singing*): "It's the wrong time . . . and the wrong place . . ."

BERNARD: No, it's the right time, and the right place!

SARAH: Are you menstruating now? Is that why you won't take your clothes off?

KARI: No.

ROBERT LEA: You should have said yes to that, it would have been easier.

JANE: Yeah, right.

BERNARD: We've got to give her an out?

M: Why? What good would that do? Supposing she was?

SARAH: I just wanted to know if she meant something specific by "the wrong time."

KARI: No, no. I didn't . . . I didn't mean that.

BERNARD: Sarah, why are you trying to give her an out? Sarah, would you answer my question?

SARAH: Uh . . . no.

BERNARD: You really weren't? Honestly?

SARAH: No, I really wasn't. That wasn't my intention.

M (*playing Sarah's* alter ego): "If I give Kari an out, then I won't have to take my clothes off either. Then I won't be the only one left with clothes on."

   Sarah laughs.

ROBERT LEA: Right, baby. That's right.

M: Yes? No?

SARAH: I'm not going to take my clothes off. Partly because now I've gotten my back up, and I'm not gonna!

KARI: Partly because you've gotten your back up?

SARAH: In fact, just because I'm stubborn.

KARI: Why?

SARAH: Why am I stubborn? Oh, my God, that's a long history!

KARI: But why do something out of stubbornness?

SARAH: Oh, I wouldn't. That's not a very good reason. But I think that because of a certain amount of pressure I've gotten into a situation now where . . . I'm not going to be forced to conform. I'm not gonna conform.

BERNARD: Sarah, you were the one who was talking before about how the whole day was a waste because you hadn't interacted enough with the group.

SARAH: I never said I thought the day was a waste. I said I would have left here disappointed if I hadn't gotten into something of my own. But this isn't *my* thing, particularly.

KARI: So what are you guys feeling now, being that we're here with our clothes on and there's all this concentration on us?

M: I'm bored with it. I want to go on and do something with the rest of us who are naked and forget about you. That's how *you* want it.

KARI: Right. Very good.

JANE: I have just one thing to say to Sarah: I think you're going to go home and wish you had.

M: And I'll say another thing to Kari: I think I understand why Sarah won't. It has to do with her being ashamed of her breasts, or her scars, or something like that. But Kari, I don't know why you're bothered, and why it's the wrong time. But you might think about it and tell us later.

SCENE 2: BODY EVALUATIONS

M: What we're going to do now is get into the feelings people have about their bodies. Each person stand up in the center of the room and everybody else will say very quickly what he or she likes the most, and the least, about this body. Then, at the end, each of you will tell us what *you* like most, and least, about your own body.

LITTLE PRINCE: Oh, wow!

> *Body Evaluation runs for well over an hour. It begins with a very noticeable focusing on arms, legs, shoulders and other "safe" areas.*
> *Bob is the first to stand up for evaluation, thus repeating the pattern he set for himself earlier, in First Impressions.*
> *As the group begins on Bob, Sarah quietly removes her clothing; Kari remains the only clothed participant.*

Bob

> *The evaluations of Bob's body echo those which were given him during First Impressions. He is, for the most part, accepted as The Average Man, built well enough*

to pass any general muster. There are no outstanding
pros or cons. He receives the group's opinions with his
usual smiling equanimity, unchallenging of anything
that is stated. Yet his tension, evinced in First Impres-
sions by slumping forward, has now drawn him to an
opposite pole: He stands stiff and erect as a military man.

BERNARD: I think you, uh . . . have a good body, but . . .

M: Bernard, if you're tempted to feel him or touch him—

BERNARD: Yeah, I know. No. I don't feel tempted to.

When the rest have given their impressions, all of which
are middle-ground ones, with neither hostile nor ex-
tremely enthusiastic content, Bob states that he likes his
shoulders best, and the center of his torso least because
he feels it is too heavy. As a younger boy, he was hung
up on his broad hips and narrow shoulders—a condition
which caused his schoolmates to joke about him. He is
grateful now that his form has changed to the acceptable
male triangle.

Yael

Yael surprises the group with a small, compact, and at-
tractive body. Special praise is given to her breasts and
nipples. Least appreciated by the group is her double
Caesarean scar, a deep ravine running from navel to
pubis. She points out other scars on her leg and foot,
left by shrapnel wounds when she was "a soldier in a
war." Of these she is most conscious of all even though
they have faded and are hardly noticeable. By the end
of her evaluation she has been praised enough to lessen
her self-doubts about her age, her body, and her gen-
eral appearance.

YAEL: I'm being told that I am well-proportioned. I didn't
believe it for many years, but now I am starting to believe it.
But I would like to be taller.

SHERSHONSKY: I think you should only wear bikinis.

YAEL: No. I'm scared to wear one.

PHILIP: I don't think you should wear a bra.

When Yael begins to make much of her shrapnel scars, the group jokes with her about her overemphasis, and she shows signs of a pleased acceptance.

Shershonsky

Shershonsky is found to be well-proportioned by average standards. Little Prince is particularly intrigued by his chest-hair pattern, which she likens to an "ink blot." Least liked are his toenails, which, due to a fungus infection, are thick and yellowed. Shershonsky says that he likes his shoulders best, but that he's "too thick in the middle."

Jane

Jane's body is thought to be beautiful, with the exception of her rather overdeveloped and protruding buttocks. Robert Lea disagrees:

ROBERT LEA: I think your body is fantastic.

JANE: Yeah, but what about my ass?

ROBERT LEA: That's to grab onto, baby!

M: Can I touch your ass?

JANE: Oh, Marty! No!

M: It surprises me. I never thought I liked big asses, but now I find it so intriguing. (*He fondles her rear.*)

BERNARD: May I do that too?

JANE: One small feel.

BERNARD: I like it.

JANE: I like my breasts best, and my ass least.

Bernard

The group compares Bernard to a Japanese Sumo *wrestler. He proves to be massive far beyond average standards, and Japanese, perhaps, in the sleekness of his skin. His thighs are immense, seeming fat at first; but on handling, the group finds them to be rocklike. There is general agreement, however, that his phallus is small, if only in proportion to the rest of his body. This criticism sets him back a bit, but he is soon able to agree. Still, there is some defensiveness left in his attitude.*

ROBERT LEA: Don't feel too bad. *I* don't feel too bad about *mine.*

PHILIP: You ought to know, Marty, the unerected state means very little as far as size . . .

BERNARD (*quickly*): That's right!

ROBERT LEA: Yeah, that's what Johnson and Masters say, don't they?

BERNARD: I like my thighs best, and my middle least. It's a little heavy.

Robert Lea

Robert Lea is found to be physically average, if a bit on the overweight side. As might be expected, his behavior and comments while standing for evaluation are wry, caustic, and sometimes flamboyantly funny. When evaluated by males, he makes the most of homosexual flippancy. In general he comes through as formerly judged: a bright, quick-witted man, happy with himself, accepting of his physical shortcomings and more free about his nudity than any of the others, with the exception of M. If his ease is partially a façade, he handles it well.

ROBERT LEA: I think my legs are best, and my ass is worst, 'cause I *have* no ass.

M: How do you shit?

ROBERT LEA: I don't shit, baby, I don't shit. (*Bernard coughs several times.*)

ROBERT LEA (*to Bernard*): Give me another blow over here. (*Laughter.*) No, don't laugh . . . Bernard is a Very Sensitive Guy. Don't fuck around with him. (*More laughter.*)

LITTLE PRINCE: I like the way your balls form a really soft bed; and a great cock. Great.

YAEL: Nothing more to add.

BERNARD (*bravely*): My eyes go to your genitals. They're like the centerpiece of the whole . . .

ROBERT LEA: This is some groovy conversation. . . .

M

M is deemed a handsome man with perhaps a bit too much weight in the buttocks. Confident, quite pleased with himself and his body, he accepts all evaluations, both pro and con, with a freedom similar to that of Robert Lea. Sarah's "most favorite" vote goes to his genitals. "Least favorite" group appraisals go to his finger, the tip of which was recently amputated by a lawnmower. But, as Robert Lea points out, "It's lucky it wasn't your prick!"

Philip

Philip, lithe, graceful, and boyish, reminds the group of Michelangelo's "David." Yet it is in his underdeveloped youthfulness that Yael and Sarah find him lacking. Special note is made of his attractive genital area (by Little Prince); and of his protruding navel, called in slang an "outsie," as opposed to the more usual "insie."

PHILIP: I like my whole body, but most my arms and hands, and least my belly button.

Sarah

The appraisals of Sarah's body are all positive, with the exception of thin shoulders, which she lets droop in a rather damaged-ego way.

BERNARD: Your Caesarean scar can't even be seen, almost. It's such a beautiful midline scar, almost imperceptible. You could wear a bikini.

SARAH: I can't wear a bikini. I've got too much . . . (*She looks down at her stomach.*)

BERNARD: I think your breasts rank with the best here.

M: If you'd throw your shoulders back, your breasts would rise at least three inches. For a woman who doesn't like saggy breasts, you'd think you'd throw your shoulders back more.

SARAH: Well, I like my breasts least, and my stomach, and what I like best is my legs.

Little Prince

As Little Prince offers herself for examination, M chooses to telephone for pizza pies, which, it turns out, cannot be delivered. The pizza call, and a discussion of what might be done about it, intrude somewhat upon the degree of attention paid to Little Prince. She is, however, far and away the most perfectly endowed of the four participating females. Her model's body is flawless and beautifully proportioned.

LITTLE PRINCE (*seeming to search deliberately for a body fault*): I don't like this . . . in here. . . .

M: Where?

LITTLE PRINCE (*looking at her waist and stomach*): The fat . . . (*Laughter. Then she slaps her rear.*)

JANE: It didn't even move!

LITTLE PRINCE: My breasts are too small.

KARI: Wow! You should see *mine!*

M: I like least the fact that your belly's so flat, from your belly button down to your pubic hair. I'd like to see more bulging. *At the completion of Body Evaluations, M throws the floor open for reactions.*

M: Let's have a little talk about what this was like for you.

BERNARD: Uh, does anybody here feel negative about it?

SARAH: I don't have any, uh . . . I don't feel negative. I feel I got some feedback that I didn't expect, so I feel better about the way I look, but I still feel very anxious and uncomfortable.

BERNARD: But not as anxious as you thought you'd feel?

SARAH: No, I think I do feel as anxious as I thought I would.

BERNARD (*with surprise*): You do?

SARAH: I did it because I felt if everybody else was going to expose him- or herself, that it really was . . . you know . . . that I should do it too.

M (*to Bernard*): Bernard, instead of taking a poll on how everyone else felt, why don't you tell us how you felt. You know, whether it was *normal* or not. (*Laughter.*)

BERNARD (*slowly, deliberately*): I would say that if someone told me at the beginning of the day that I would have to get up and stand in front of everybody, one by one, and get an opinion about my body, I would never have believed it.

YAEL: Marty, close the window, some of us are cold.

M: Yael, why don't you just say, "*I* am cold."

YAEL: *I* am cold. (*She goes for the sheet and wraps it around herself.*)

BERNARD (*continuing*): It's incredible that I could do this without feeling the least bit of . . . uh, I felt no anxiety whatsoever. I felt nothing but good things about it.

SHERSHONSKY: Uh, I'm really surprised that you said that because I would think, you know, that you're running around with your clothes off anytime, uh, and you wouldn't give a shit.

ROBERT LEA: I would never have thought that.

JANE: I wouldn't either.

ROBERT LEA (*to Bernard*): No, we don't know you at all. From here we get the impression that it's your desire to run around with your clothes off all the time. But I don't think you're fucking every girl you'd like to fuck, which probably hangs you up. Actually, you're in bed with your wife most of the time; maybe once or twice a year with another girl. No . . . I don't imagine you're running around with your clothes off all the time. . . .

M: Okay, now that you've finished with him, what do you want to tell us about *you*?

ROBERT LEA: Me? What do I want to tell you about me?

M: Yeah. So far you're only running down Bernard.

> *Robert Lea persists in focusing on Bernard; the argument, while controlled, has undercurrents of hostility. Lea feels that M is egging them on.*

ROBERT LEA (*to M*): I think you're looking for more combat. You want my other head to get hurt.

M: I take it back. But I'd like to say something about you instead of your talking about Bernard. You're very cool. You handle yourself in every situation. Nothing bugs you. But you were more bugged by standing up there and being judged than by anything else. I know, because you joked so well about it.

ROBRERT LEA: Oh, I joke about everything.

BOB: I agree. I think you were obviously using your intellect and quick wit to cover up because you didn't have the clothes to cover up with anymore.

ROBERT LEA: I was doing that when I was dressed, too, wasn't I?

BOB: Not nearly as much.

SARAH: No, not nearly as much.

M: I wonder if your dislike about yourself was that your cock wasn't big enough.

ROBERT LEA: It gets big enough when it has to get big.

M: Oh.

ROBERT LEA: My ass should be bigger.

After a pause, Little Prince begins a long discussion based on her body hang-up: the neurotic dichotomy between her desire for a perfect body and her malaise about stressing physicality. She adds that while she has always been a perfectionist, she is now learning, through the marathon, that people's bodies are beautiful in their uniqueness rather than in their perfection.

BERNARD: Didn't you love all the adulation we gave you about your body? You seemed to be enjoying it.

LITTLE PRINCE: No . . . I was . . .

BERNARD: For the first time today you really looked very happy while you were standing up there.

LITTLE PRINCE: Well, you're wrong. I was very anxious. *Very.*

YAEL: I agree with Bernard. I thought that you were very happy.

LITTLE PRINCE: Well, it's better than having people say you're awful, you're ugly . . . but it made me very nervous. But you don't believe me, do you . . . ?

JANE: No. Now that it's over, how do you feel?

LITTLE PRINCE: Uh . . . I'm glad that people enjoyed me, because I enjoyed them . . . but I don't know . . . I'm really confused about it, and I hate talking about it now because I feel very uncomfortable.

BERNARD: I am bitterly disappointed that Kari didn't take her clothes off.

M (*to Kari*): Did you ever figure out why you didn't want to?

KARI: Yeah. It seems really stupid now that I am, uh . . . shy and embarrassed about my body. . . . I'll get into a bikini this summer, and I feel I have too small breasts, and, uh . . . inverted nipples . . . and I am heavy, and my thighs. . . . (*She begins to ramble.*)

M: You mean if you ever get it into a more perfect state, you would then show it to us?

KARI: No, no, no, no . . . I'll never be perfect because I have thick ankles, I have peasant legs . . . I don't. . . .

SHERSHONSKY: Do you think you would lose a great deal by doing it?

KARI: Uh . . . I don't know . . .

M: I'll tell you this: Just as with talking, ninety percent of the stuff you do is useless, and ten percent is useful. Now, one of the things you get in the kind of thing we just did is that you realize the arbitrariness of certain body things. Everybody always has something he doesn't want to show and doesn't like, like "My breasts are too big," or "My breasts are too small," or "My scars are awful," or "My prick's too small." But then you find out that someone else will like just what you thought was so terrible. What you're willing to accept or reject is a totally arbitrary thing. There's nothing absolute about it. There's no such thing as a big ass that is, in itself, awful. Someone else might groove on a big ass. So you might as well *choose* to accept your body rather than be uncomfortable about it.

KARI (*to Jane*): But still, I'll bet you'll never accept your big ass, no matter who else likes it.

JANE: Right. David loves my big ass, but I still hate it.

KARI: Right.

JANE: But the gain for me is now knowing I can do it. Like Bernard, if I had known this morning that I'd have to stand up in front of everybody stark naked, I would have said, Forget it! But now I know I can do it. Having someone say your ass is too big doesn't destroy you. . . . (*She laughs.*)

M (*to Kari*): See, so *you* might have gotten that out of it. It's up to you: If you want to now, fine; if you don't want to, that's up to you.

KARI (*after a pause*): I don't really want to.

SCENE 3: TAKE A WALK

M: Do you want to do something different now?

SARAH: Yeah. I want to get dressed. (*Laughter.*)

M: Think of the person you think is least useful to you in this room, and ask him to leave, to walk outside. Then tell us why you asked him to leave, and then bring him back in. The person you think you like least, or the one who has made the least contribution.

Bob asks Bernard to leave.

BOB: I think that Bernard is in many ways diametrically opposed to me. He's extremely competitive, whereas I'm not. He's aggressive and violent, which are both characteristics which I reject.

Bob brings Bernard back. Jane asks Philip to leave.

JANE: I pick Philip because as far as I'm concerned Philip hasn't been in there at all. He hasn't opened himself, he hasn't taken any risk, he hasn't that I can recall said anything to me that meant anything to me. I mean, you know, at times I've completely forgotten he's here. With the exception of Little Prince he just hasn't related to anybody.

M: Okay, go get him.

SHERSHONSKY: I was going to ask Kari to leave.

Kari leaves.

SHERSHONSKY: I asked Kari to leave because she's not esthetically pleasing to me, and because she's very firm and set. Like you can't communicate with her. Not only not taking clothing off, but other things too.

SARAH: I pick Philip.

Kari returns. Philip begins to leave again.

SARAH: Philip is the only one I didn't have anything to do with. It's partly my fault too, but he's the one person that didn't reach out to me. Everyone else has been of use to me in one way or another.

Philip returns.

YAEL: Philip, I choose. Poor Philip.

PHILIP: I'll *stay* out. (*He leaves for the third time.*)

ROBERT LEA: He'll never come back.

YAEL: I almost wanted to change my mind, but I couldn't. Except that he smiles a few times, I didn't get a feeling of who-who-who he is. And he made me feel very old. . . . (*She laughs self-consciously.*)

Philip reenters.

BERNARD: I choose M.

ROBERT LEA: That's right, pick the King. Strong Guy. (*Laughter.*)

M leaves.

BERNARD (*grandly*): Lock the door! I don't completely trust M. At times I get the feeling of insincerity, about fifty percent of the time, and I wanted to tell everybody.

M returns munching a sandwich.

KARI: Robert Lea . . .

He leaves.

KARI: He's just the one in the room that, as a man . . . he threatens me. I don't know how to reach to him, to touch . . . I don't trust my reactions. . . .

M: What are your reactions?

KARI: . . . I feel very isolated from his type of man.

LITTLE PRINCE: Bernard.

Bernard leaves.

M: Why, Little Prince?

LITTLE PRINCE: I didn't ask him to leave because he's useless. But he's a person who baffles me. His type of thinking frightens me, and even though he kissed me before, I don't feel I could relate to him except in trying to please. *I* was useless . . . that kind of martyr thing which is very difficult for me.

Bernard returns.

M: Who else hasn't chosen? Philip?

PHILIP: Um . . . it's hard for me to pick out anyone. In fact, I'd like you *all* to leave.

The group rises and begins to file out, laughing.

PHILIP: No, come back! Hey! I don't believe this is happening!

Little Prince stays behind.

LITTLE PRINCE: Why did you want them to leave?

She and Philip sit very close to each other, arms entwined, making a scene of quiet, gentle love. Their youthful nakedness forms a momentary idyll. Their whisperings are inaudible.

After several minutes, Philip calls, and the group returns.

M: I wasn't going to pick anybody, but I think I'll pick Little Prince and Philip.

They leave together.

M: I asked Little Prince to leave because of the histrionics, and Philip because of the lack of exposing himself. And I think they'll be happy together.

They reenter.

ROBERT LEA: I didn't pick anyone because I really like all of you. Like . . . stay, and enjoy.

M: But if you had to pick someone?

ROBERT LEA: I couldn't. I like got a little thing going with everybody. Obviously, not with Kari. *She* chased *me* out.

M: Pick in spite of it.

ROBERT LEA (*after some argument with M*): Bob.

Bob leaves.

ROBERT LEA: I asked him to leave because he's just a "nice guy"— that's all. In this world there's not enough room for "nice guys." He really seems tuned out of this whole thing.

BERNARD: He's too nice.

ROBERT LEA: Like he just got married a month ago, so he's gonna go home and tell his wife, like, "Nothing happened. Don't worry, baby, nothing's changed between us."

Bob returns.

BERNARD: I want to thank all of you who didn't send me out. (*Laughter.*)

M: You got three votes, right?

BERNARD: Little Prince sent me out, and Philip sent me out with the rest of you. Two.

YAEL: With the rest?

KARI: You've got to count that too?

M: You side with the negative.

BERNARD: Can we ask why people sent us out?

M: Sure, talk about it.

KARI (*to Shershonsky*): Yeah. Why did you pick me?

SHERSHONSKY (*with difficulty and hesitance*): Uh . . . um . . . I'm not physically attracted to you . . . and I have a feeling you're kind of rigid. . . .

M (*to Bernard*): When you asked me to leave I thought it was groovy to go out and eat without missing anything. I mean, I was still part of it. And I thought too that maybe you'd get some clarity in your head, or you'd see the fact that maybe I didn't feel like busting your head in before, or making any competition with you.

BERNARD (*after a pause*): Can I ask why Little Prince threw me out?

LITTLE PRINCE: I didn't think I could relate to you, although you kissed me. And your ideas baffle me . . . I mean . . . the necessity of hitting people over the head.

BERNARD: Do you feel I betrayed you, I kissed you and then later I didn't behave toward you the way I should?

LITTLE PRINCE: No, no, not at all! (*She looks to M:*) I'd like to know why you chose Philip. I . . . I knew you'd choose me. It wasn't easy for me, but I feel it was good I had to leave the room, and I'm interested in why.

M: I think you've all been useful to me, but I chose Philip because I know least about him. I thought of you first, but then I didn't want to pick you, because after all, you went out in the park, and when you came back you went through something. You did more things than Philip. But then when Philip sent everyone out, it clicked, and I felt you two had something going between you, so I sent you both out together. In a sense I feel deprived that I didn't get to know you two better. There was something exclusive between you, and you didn't bring much to other people. I felt, for instance, that the two of you could have met on the street, or anywhere, and you'd have had the same thing. The other eight people were expendable.

JANE: Yeah. If I had known I could have sent out two people, I'd have picked both of you for the same reasons as Marty said. You had that whole breakdown thing, but then you completely withdrew.

LITTLE PRINCE: That's exposing, though.

JANE: How's that exposing? You just stayed in the clubhouse.

SCENE 4: THE FORCING OF PHILIP

PHILIP: I wasn't really put to anything. I'm not the kind of person who volunteers a whole lot about myself that's deep, but if put to it, you know, I'll respond.

M: We didn't force you enough?

PHILIP: Right. I'm very passive, probably.

BERNARD: I think that's a nice understatement.

ROBERT LEA: People can take from you, but you can't give.

PHILIP: Well . . . I give also. . . .

LITTLE PRINCE (*in defense of Philip*): I disagree with that, but that's personal.

ROBERT LEA (*cynically*): You mean you know him so well?

LITTLE PRINCE (*coughing*): No . . . but from the entire day, I think he has given to me.

M (*to Philip*): How can we force you?

PHILIP: Uh . . . ask me questions.

SHERSHONSKY: Rock him.

ROBERT LEA: He could be very uncomplicated, Marty. Maybe there isn't anything there to get.

PHILIP: What do you mean by that?

> *M goes over to Philip and pulls him out of his chair by the hair.*

SHERSHONSKY: Stop it! God!

M (*to Philip*): Talk!

PHILIP: Well . . . you know I'm not going to talk unless you . . .

M: Unless I force you.

BERNARD (*to Philip, perhaps to M*): Kick him in the balls.

ROBERT LEA: Oh, Marty, cut it out, man! Cut it out!

PHILIP (*smiling sheepishly*): Ask me questions.

> *M relaxes his grip on Philip's hair, drapes his arm around his shoulder, and walks with him around the circle, stopping first in front of Sarah.*

SARAH: What makes you feel out of it here?

PHILIP: I don't feel out of it. I really . . . uh . . . felt that I had a thing with just about everybody. . . . I like everyone a lot.

SARAH: Does it have anything to do with your being younger than the rest of us?

PHILIP: Yeah . . . I feel that.

SARAH: Are you in awe of us, or put off?

PHILIP: In awe? I don't think so.

ROBERT LEA: Do you distrust anybody here? Wouldn't you like to make a friend here?

PHILIP: Yeah . . . uh . . . I'd like to meet everyone again.

ROBERT LEA: Do you find everyone honest?

PHILIP: Uh . . . yeah, I do.

ROBERT LEA: No dishonesty at all?

PHILIP: I can't . . . uh . . . I couldn't . . . uh . . . on the whole everyone's been beautiful.

JANE: Did you have a risk?

PHILIP (*still tending to smile uncomfortably*): Not really.

JANE: If you had one now, what would the risk be?

PHILIP: Uh . . . I can't think of anything that would make me anxious. . . .

LITTLE PRINCE: Yes, you can. What about your girlfriend? Suppose she sleeps with somebody else tonight. You get back and she walks in at three o'clock in the morning.

PHILIP: Oh.

LITTLE PRINCE: Would you be anxious?

PHILIP: I'd be very upset.

LITTLE PRINCE: Why? Is your intensity explosive?

M (*cutting her off*): One question. I gave you three because I know you like to ask a lot of questions.

YAEL (*to Philip*): I feel very warm. I like your smile, especially. But I want to ask you if you felt about me that, you know, it's an older generation, and they've had it.

PHILIP: I, uh . . . couldn't place you as far as generation goes. Uh, you've got one foot in Jane's generation, and then you've got one foot in Sarah's maybe. . . .

SARAH: What generation is that? (*Laughter.*)

PHILIP: You can have your choice.

BERNARD: The Lost Generation.

SHERSHONSKY: What have you learned about yourself from today that you didn't know when you came?

PHILIP: Well . . . I . . . I learned that I can be very free and un-
anxious about being undressed.

> *Kari asks Philip about his teeth. He explains that he had
> a diving-board accident at the age of eight, knocked out
> his two top front teeth, and has been wearing a tempo-
> rary bridge ever since, which is now about to be changed
> to a permanent one. Kari latches on to the details and
> questions him at length.*

BOB *(to Philip)*: I'd like to know what made it so difficult for
you to open up during the seven or eight different exercises
we've had so far, and why it's necessary for you to be escorted
around the room and have people throw questions at you for
you to respond.

PHILIP: Well . . . uh . . . Wasn't everybody else responding to
questions too?

BOB: I think people respond to questions after they've opened
up a little first.

PHILIP: Well, I wasn't completely closed.

M *(as Philip's alter ego)*: "I'm copping to my passive feelings,
and I thought it would help if people came and helped me
pull out of it. I'd like to come out of it."

PHILIP: True.

M *(continuing)*: "It might seem silly to you, but it makes sense
to me."

PHILIP: True.

BERNARD: I must say I didn't think they still made people like
you. I, uh, think you're a sweet, gentle soul, and, uh, I have
nothing but positive feelings about you.

M: I'm very sorry I pulled your hair.

PHILIP: That's okay.

M: I think it was the wrong thing to do.

PHILIP: I don't think I lost very much, and I'm glad you see . . .
It wasn't the wrong idea, you know.

ROBERT LEA: You're a nice cat. You couldn't do any harm.

PHILIP: What do you mean by that?

M: You mean you're not such a nice cat, and people like you can be misjudged?

ROBERT LEA (*ignoring M's remark*): This is a very nice cat, and he wouldn't want to hurt anyone.

PHILIP: Anyone . . . ?

M (*as Philip's alter ego*): "You're crazy if you think I wouldn't want to hurt anybody."

PHILIP (*nodding*): Oh, I've hurt people.

ROBERT LEA: Out of being defensive?

PHILIP: No. Many times, unintentionally . . .

ROBERT LEA: Unintentionally. Well, that's what I mean. You couldn't do it deliberately.

PHILIP: Well, it's very tricky. Things that you think are unintentional are really sometimes intentional. Uh, you don't mean to do them, but nevertheless you do. . . .

ROBERT LEA: All right, you're bad!

Philip laughs and gives Robert Lea a quick smile.

SCENE 5: THE BODY CHESS GAME

ROBERT LEA: I want to know why Kari sent me out.

KARI: Well, because, uh . . . you're threatening to me. As a man, you're threatening.

ROBERT LEA: How do I threaten you?

M: Listen, the reasons she gave when you were out weren't clear to me either. So I'd like to have another nonverbal thing. We'll do it a little differently, instead of just having you talk to each other. We'll play it out like chess. You want to know what she means, but I don't think she can tell you any better

than she told us. I think she fools herself with words. So we'll
do this chess game. Each one of you makes one move at a
time, in any direction. Then you freeze, and the other makes
a move. The game isn't over until both of you want to stop.

BERNARD: What about physical contact?

M: Oh, sure. That too.

> *The Chess Game between the nude Robert Lea and Kari,
> clothed, is enacted as follows:*
>
> *One move at a time, they near each other. Lea seems bent
> on a direct, head-on meeting, but Kari counters each ad-
> vance with a side step. Two more steps apiece, and they
> have passed, untouching. He tries again to confront her.
> At times, she changes her strategy and moves toward
> him, encouraging him to confront her again. When he
> does, she sidesteps. He thrusts forward; she moves back.
> One more forward step, and suddenly she turns her back
> to him. Now he places his hands on her waist from be-
> hind and tries to draw her close. She bows her head; then
> pushes him away with considerable force.*

ROBERT LEA: All right. That's it.

M: Is it any clearer to you now?

ROBERT LEA: It's not very clear. No.

M: Do you want to talk to him about it? Don't psychoanalyze,
just tell each other what you felt within yourselves.

> *Kari stares down at the floor.*

M: As I said before, Kari, you want contact with people, so see
if you can look at him while you talk.

KARI: Ah . . . I don't like the feel . . .

ROBERT LEA: Uh, what's the feeling? I don't know how you feel.

KARI: Ah, well . . . I don't like your games.

ROBERT LEA: What games?

KARI: Of all the people here, I feel you play the biggest game.

M (*as her alter ego*): "I feel you are playing games with me."
> *She nods.*

ROBERT LEA: What game was I playing with you?

KARI: You were playing it not only with me.

ROBERT LEA: Why should you care what I was playing with other people?

KARI: You were playing it with me too.

ROBERT LEA: What was I doing to upset you?

KARI: First of all, the sex part of it, which is a man, and that is what I call a threat. It's very animalistic. It scares me, because it comes, it draws from all sources. Ah . . . uh . . . it's not to me predictable. I can't even key in on it. Does that make sense?

M (as her alter ego): "I'm frightened of your sexuality."

KARI: Yeah. Your sexuality scares me. . . . And I'll fight it. I guess that's how I'll combat it.

ROBERT LEA: You like someone who's very passive to see if you can seduce him?

KARI: No.

ROBERT LEA: You like to be seduced?

KARI: Uh . . . yeah.

M: Tell him what frightens you about his sexuality.

KARI: It is that I'm afraid you can make it without me.

ROBERT LEA: I don't understand that.

KARI: I mean you don't need me to get your kicks.

ROBERT LEA: You in particular?

KARI: Me, or girls, or—

M (as her alter ego): "I would like to feel you couldn't make it without me."

KARI: Right.

M (continuing): "I would like to feel you're interested in me."

KARI: Right. You're the kind of person that I don't dent, or I don't make any impression either good, bad, or indifferent. It doesn't matter what I do or say or feel. It doesn't move you.

ROBERT LEA: Did you really want to move me?

KARI: I would like to move every man, I think.

ROBERT LEA: But me in particular?

KARI: No. But I didn't move you.

M (*as her alter ego again*): "I'm kind of attracted to you, but it doesn't mean anything if you're just sexual with everybody."

KARI: No, that's not true, Marty.

She looks at Bernard, then speaks again to Robert Lea.

KARI: I could pick Bernard, but he's not as complex as you. He's got the same aggressions going as you, but with you it's mental and emotional, and—

ROBERT LEA: Well, what is there if it's not mental and emotional? How else are you going to get to know—

KARI: With you it's complex.

ROBERT LEA: No. Mental and emotional. I function on those two levels very securely. I don't know any other level to function on, and if you're going to function emotionally, it has to be primitive.

M: Tell her how you felt during the whole exercise.

ROBERT LEA: I felt like just grabbing her, and getting to know her physically. And she knew it, and she didn't want me to. (*To Kari:*) Why didn't you want me to grab you?

KARI: I didn't know you wanted to. You were confused, you didn't really know what was going on with me, yet you persisted with the sexuality.

ROBERT LEA: And you were very hostile toward me.

KARI: But doesn't that make you curious?

ROBERT LEA: Certainly, I was curious.

KARI: But that doesn't stand in the way of your sex impulse for me, right?

ROBERT LEA: Right. But I don't think you got to know your own sexual impulses. You turn yourself off even before you can get yourself turned on.

KARI: It's true, sometimes, for certain types of men.

ROBERT LEA: You're very, very defensive.

KARI: It's true.

ROBERT LEA: Are you afraid that I would probably turn you on?

KARI: No.

ROBERT LEA: I couldn't do that?

KARI: Yes, maybe, but not now. Maybe one day when I get to understand you and don't feel you as a threat. . . . Because I wouldn't want to be raped.

ROBERT LEA: I would never rape you.

KARI: I might like to get seduced, but not raped, and not by you.

ROBERT LEA: You wouldn't have to worry about that. I would like you to rape me, though.

The discussion continues, and Kari's fear of Robert Lea's sexuality becomes even more apparent. She is also fearful, it would seem, of her own. The group tends to side with Lea, pointing out that his advances were slow and respectful and that, to a degree, she did lead him on, only to reject him.

BERNARD: I must say I was very impressed with Robert Lea's resiliency and confidence and refusal to be intimidated by being rebuffed. To me this represents total insensitivity— (*The group laughs heartily, but Bernard continues in dead earnest.*) Well, it *does.* Or else it indicates an enormous feeling of security in going through with this game without being humiliated by the rebuff. I was also curious why Kari chose *me* to insult so much when I wasn't even involved in this game. Did anyone notice that?

SHERSHONSKY: In what way?

BERNARD: She said the only difference between him and me is that he's more complex than I am. So I got all the shit, *plus* what he got. . . . (*The group begins to laugh again.*) I wasn't even involved in this, so I got curious, and a little depressed. . . .

YAEL (*to Robert Lea*): I was worried she would smack you one!

ROBERT LEA: I was, also.

KARI (*giggling*): Were you?
YAEL: I thought, "Another second and she'll hit him!"

SCENE 6: THE QUICK TURN-ON

M: Anyone want a quick turn-on?
ROBERT LEA: Yeah.
M: Okay. Think of something you'd like to hear.
ROBERT LEA: Oh, I thought you meant some pot.
M: No, no. Think of something you'd like to hear, that you'd really groove on hearing.
YAEL: I don't want to hear anything anymore, I just want to be hugged.

> *The entire group hugs Yael, all trying to get part of her at the same time. She continues to hold the sheet about her and is assailed by loving naked bodies.*

PHILIP: She thinks we're going to kill her! (*He laughs.*)
YAEL: No! That was beautiful!
ROBERT LEA: Just think of this experience at home, and that'll turn you on!
M: How do you feel?

> *Yael answers with a small shrieking sound.*

M: Kari, what would you like to hear?
KARI: That you all like me even though I didn't take my clothes off. . . .

> *The sentence "Kari, I really like you even though you didn't take your clothes off" is repeated separately by M, Sarah, Little Prince, Philip, Jane, Bob.*

ROBERT LEA: Kari, I like you even though you didn't take your clothes off because I can really see you without your clothes.

YAEL: Kari, the nicest thing you could do is take your clothes off.

BERNARD: Kari, I'd like you better if you took your clothes off.

SARAH: I'd like everybody to say to me, "Sarah, please put your clothes on." (*Laughter.*)

> *The group complies by repeating the sentence, but Sarah makes no move to dress.*
>
> *Philip, with his long Hippie coiffure, asks to be told, "Philip, your hair is too short."*
>
> *He beams.*
>
> *Bob wishes to be told, "Bob, you're a good friend."*

ROBERT LEA: I'd like to hear what you would like to tell me—very quickly, in one pithy statement.

BERNARD: You're full of shit.

BOB: I don't think I got through to you.

KARI: I didn't either.

PHILIP: You're a quarter full of shit, only a quarter.

LITTLE PRINCE: I know you may not be in the hip world, but I think sometimes you put it on pretty well.

YAEL: I think I would like to meet you and talk to you a little more.

SHERSHONSKY: I like you.

JANE: Robert E. Lea, I like you.

SARAH: I'd like to know you better. I think I had a feeling that you put on some of this Hippie stuff, too. But I think there's a lot behind that, and I wish I knew it.

M: I think you're a groovy guy.

YAEL (*half joking, half in anguish*): We'll be here for a week. . . .

LITTLE PRINCE (*after a pause*): What do you all think I am? Tell me it's okay to be who I am, even if you disagree with it.

M: I think you're hysterical, but it's okay to be hysterical.

BERNARD: I have to think. . . .

BOB: I think you have a good body, and it's all right to have a good body.

KARI: I think you try, and I love that.

PHILIP: I think you're a girl, and it's fine that you're a girl.

YAEL: I think you're charming, and I-I-I would hope that you get over some of these difficulties.

M: And it's okay to be charming.

SHERSHONSKY: I think you're a great guy, and I hope you get through into nice things.

JANE: I think you're too self-indulgent, and it's okay to be too self-indulgent.

ROBERT LEA: You're a nice young thing, and I hope you straighten yourself out.

M: And it's okay to be a nice young thing.

ROBERT LEA: And it's okay to be unstraight, too.

SARAH: I think you're a little princess, and it's okay to be a little princess.

BERNARD: You're the kind of girl who twelve years ago I would have fallen head over heels in love with, but I can't indulge myself in that type of girl anymore. But I think that, corny as it sounds, you have all the assets to see you through life very happily if you can somehow put them all together and use them properly.

SHERSHONSKY: I'd like every girl in the room to say, "Shershonsky, hang loose, you're going to make it."

The five girls repeat the sentence, adding, "And it's okay if you don't."

M (*looking at Sarah, who is still naked*): Put your clothes on, Sarah.

SARAH: Now that I've got them off, I don't want to put them on. (*Laughter.*)

M (*looking at Little Prince*): I think you're a beautiful picture of a woman, sitting there with your labia exposed. I don't know why women sit with their legs crossed. . . . Now I'll tell you what I would like people to tell me. "M, I've really gotten something out of this evening, and I'll try to put it to use in the weeks ahead."

The group repeats the sentence in unison. M grins happily.

KARI: There's an egomaniac for you. . . .

On Jane's request, the group tells her, "Jane, I'm really glad I met you." Now everyone has had a turn.

PHILIP (*to M*): What's next in your bag of tricks?

YAEL: Sarah should get another chance because she didn't put the clothes on when she asked for it.

SARAH: I felt better when people said that. Now that I have my clothes next to me I don't feel like putting them on.

M: I like this procedure because it shows again how people say, "I don't want to ask for something because then if I get it it won't have any meaning—it's not legitimate." Yet it never fails that when you say, "Tell me this," whether you believe it or not, it sounds great. (*There is much laughter from the others.*)

JANE: Really. It really does.

M: So what is all this shit about not saying what you want, when getting it feels so good?

SARAH: The reason I didn't ask for anything profound was that I really don't feel there is anything I can ask somebody and they would give me under those conditions . . . uh . . . that would feel good.

JANE: Yeah, but didn't it feel good when we told you to put your clothes on?

SARAH: Yeah, that felt nice, sure, but you know . . .

M: How about trying "Sarah, you're a beautiful woman."

SARAH (*quietly*): Okay. Say, "Sarah, you're a beautiful woman" . . . (*and then adds loudly*) The men!

Each man, separately, repeats the statement.

M: How does it feel?

SARAH: It feels nice.

BERNARD: Was it really nice?

SARAH (*quietly again*): Yes. . . . At first I was thinking, "I don't believe you." But then a lot of you sounded as if you meant it, and so it really felt . . . But the thing is, if you ask somebody to say what you want to hear, then they've got to say it whether they feel it or not.

M: Still, it feels nice to hear it.

SARAH: Well, but—

BERNARD: Who wants to get rocked?

SARAH: Do you want to get rocked, Bernard?

BERNARD (*flustered*): Uh . . . I feel inhibited about it for some reason. Maybe I did want to be . . . but I'm not so sure now. . . .

SHERSHONSKY: There hasn't been a man rocked, just the girls.

M (*to Bernard*): We've got a little less than two hours to go, so if you feel you want to, this is your chance. But, it's not a man's thing to do, is it, Bernard . . . ?

BERNARD: I'll expose my hang-up. . . .

M (*drily*): Terrible.

KARI: We only have two hours to go?

M: About.

KARI: How come I got a feeling like we're saying good-bye?

LITTLE PRINCE: Because we had a really good thing, maybe.

PHILIP: It's going to be a long good-bye.

KARI (*with relief*): A long good-bye. That's kind of nice too.

SARAH: I've got a feeling, which I may be projecting, that everyone's so tired it's kind of played out.

BERNARD: Yeah.

SHERSHONSKY: I disagree. I feel very, uh, alert and alive.

BERNARD: Who . . . who wants to go home right now?

PHILIP: I feel like I've been to sleep and it's Sunday already.

SARAH: I don't feel like going home. I was going to ask Marty if he had any second-wind techniques.

m: We can open the windows. Do you want to jump up and
down?

scene 7: help someone

m: Now let's try a help thing. If there's someone here you'd
like to help, sit down with them and try to help them. We'll
give you three to five minutes.

BERNARD (*after a long pause*): Okay. Robert Lea.

ROBERT LEA: Holy shit!

YAEL (*amid a roar of group laughter*): Bernard, you're great!
*Bernard and Robert Lea sit in the center of the floor,
facing each other.*

BERNARD (*to Robert Lea*): The problem with you is—

KARI: Oh, shoot!

BERNARD (*looking at her*): And I'm coming to you *next!* (*To
Lea:*) You're not capitalizing on your assets.

ROBERT LEA: Which are?

BERNARD: Your main asset is akin to a sense of humor, a willingness to laugh at yourself. Your least appealing trait is a tendency to become slightly pompous, and to try to impress people.
But despite all the bullshit, you're still one of the people
here whom I'd like to have a friendship with.

ROBERT LEA: You're wild. Thank you.

BERNARD: What happens is, every so often you start taking
yourself serious, and you drive people away. So this is, uh,
the advice I have for you—

ROBERT LEA (*with sarcasm*): Thank you, doctor. What do I owe
you for this visit? I like myself and I function very well in
the society in which I am an inhabitant, and I find that

people with whom I associate like me.

BERNARD: So what?

ROBERT LEA: It's not what you mentioned just now. I don't take myself seriously at all. I'm really very frivolous and capricious and lighthearted and light-headed.

BERNARD: Okay.

ROBERT LEA: And amiable and lovely. (*He pauses.*) And *lovely*.

BERNARD: Yeah.

ROBERT LEA: Okay.

BERNARD: Yeah.

ROBERT LEA: You really helped me.

M: Are you being facetious?

ROBERT LEA: No.

M: Tell him how he helped you.

ROBERT LEA (*to Bernard*): You showed me that you really don't dislike me as much as I thought you did. I like you. But I don't think we could ever really be good friends. We would probably run into a lot of conflict. . . . But . . . you don't give a shit.

M: Is that true, Bernard, that you don't give a shit?

Bernard has been walking away from Lea, looking down at the floor.

BERNARD: Um . . . I didn't want to hear what he was saying anymore.

M: Because he told you he couldn't be friends?

BERNARD: I would have preferred him to say nothing, maybe just thought about what I said.

BOB: I'd like to help Kari. First of all, I'd like to say that of all the women here I think you're the most beautiful. But not only aren't you able to express things verbally, you even find it difficult physically. But there's something there that a lot of us would like to share. In the beginning I criticized you for being distrustful and standoffish. But I think you have to keep trying to get past that.

LITTLE PRINCE: Can I do two short little things with people?

M: One.

LITTLE PRINCE (*going over to Sarah*): I wanted to tell you I thought you were beautiful. And because you don't know what you want to receive from people, I want to give you something that I like, and that makes me happy, because you were so nice to me. I don't know if you're going to like this, but just let me do it, okay?

SARAH: Okay.

> *Little Prince takes out of her bag a small box of paste eye shadow and begins to paint something on Sarah's cheek with her finger.*

LITTLE PRINCE: It's just a little flower, and it reminds me of spring and love and warmth and giving, and all that means.

ROBERT LEA (*looking at it*): Oh, it *is* nutty. . . .

SARAH (*at the door mirror*): Oh, I like that! (*She laughs affectionately.*)

M: It's very pretty.

YAEL: Yes, it's very pretty.

SARAH: Gee, that's very skillful, the way you drew it.

LITTLE PRINCE (*softly*): Thank you. Little Princes have many talents. . . .

M: Hey, Little Prince, will you draw something on me too?

> *She begins to decorate his bare shoulders with eye-shadow flowers.*

M: Beautiful!

PHILIP: I'd like to help Bernard. Bernard, would you like my advice?

BERNARD: Yeah.

PHILIP: I sort of feel sad about you. About your old age. Uh, you deny yourself so much. There's a whole tremendous world that you don't let yourself experience. Uh, by limiting relationships, you lose so much. . . .

BERNARD: Say, I don't want to leave everyone with the impression that all I'm interested in is fucking girls and beating guys at tennis. . . .

PHILIP: I think you should follow your fantasies and desires and whims.

SARAH: Except for that one to be normal!

BERNARD: That's very nice of you to want to help me. Most people want to send me out of the room. . . .

M: There you go siding with the negative. Jesus Christ, are you keeping that vote list?

BERNARD (*laughing*): It's pretty sad. I'm going to tell my wife that only three people present thought I was obnoxious!

M (*smiling at Little Prince*): "As Joseph Goebbels said . . ." if you repeat a lie often enough, everyone will start to believe it. And you're doing very dangerous things with yourself, Bernard. Try to hold onto the vote when you're talking about what most people think of you.

BERNARD (*after a thoughtful pause*): Do you think it would be possible . . . do you think it would be all right if we held that vote again just before we leave later? But only by secret ballot.

The request is granted by M. Bernard closes his eyes. The vote is taken, and the results are: Nine, not obnoxious; one, obnoxious.

M: You can't win 'em all.

YAEL: He looks happier, he really looks happier now.

BERNARD: I'm really, uh . . . curious about who the one is . . .

LITTLE PRINCE: Oh, you're really fucking with it!

ROBERT LEA: Who do you think it was? We're not going to tell you if you're right or wrong, but you can try to guess.

BERNARD (*looking at Marjorie sitting in the hall*): If she could vote, it would probably be her, but she can't vote. . . .

SARAH: Why can't she vote?

ROBERT LEA: She hasn't paid her poll tax.

MARJORIE: May I tell him if he's right or wrong?

M: No.

MARJORIE: Shit.

BERNARD: It was you, wasn't it?

M: No, you just sit with it, Bernard. What the hell.

MARJORIE (*resignedly*): So let it bother him.

M: Let it bother him. (*To Bernard:*) You're entitled to let that one no vote fuck up the other nine.

MARJORIE: But it's fucking *me* up!

LITTLE PRINCE: Well, that's *your* bit.

M: Right. That's your bit.

KARI: Gee, I like to hear her voice. I haven't heard it all this time. Aren't you going out of your mind a bit?

MARJORIE: Yes. I am. (*Laughter.*)

KARI: Can't you come in and join us?

PHILIP: You could take your clothes off and join us.

MARJORIE: *I cannot* take my clothes off. (*She begins to explain that the prohibition is based on her position as observer-reporter.*)

M: Keep out of it. Take them off or sit there quietly.

MARJORIE: Stop shutting me up! I've been shut up for sixteen hours!

KARI: Sixteen hours . . . !

M makes a loud humming sound which quiets everyone.

SCENE 8: HE LOVES ME NOT

M places a swivel chair in the center of the room.

M: Each one of you, one at a time, will sit here, and everybody else will tell you very pithily, in one short sentence, something he dislikes about you.

Shershonsky

BOB: I dislike your uncertainty.

KARI: I dislike your reaction to me, and your hesitation.

PHILIP: I dislike your choice of a name.

LITTLE PRINCE: I dislike your lack of hope that you'll love.

YAEL: I dislike that you didn't put your arm around me when I was sitting next to you.

JANE: I dislike that you put yourself down.

ROBERT LEA: I dislike the fact that you attempt to elicit sympathy.

M: I dislike that you can't tell people you like them, or can't touch them.

BERNARD: I dislike your compulsion to make everybody like you, to make them feel good.

SARAH: I dislike your distance.

Sarah

ROBERT LEA: I dislike that you're sad.

JANE: I dislike that you're sad too.

SHERSHONSKY: I dislike that you seem so passive about yourself.

YAEL: I dislike that you said "loneliness." And I don't feel that you have a spirit of fighting, to do something about it.

PHILIP: I dislike your reluctance to smile.

KARI: I dislike your confirmations . . . your, uh . . . con—

BOB: I dislike your resignation to your situation.

BERNARD: I can't think of anything I dislike about you.

LITTLE PRINCE: I dislike that you don't rejoice about yourself enough.

M: I dislike your not asking for what you want more vigorously.

SARAH: Everybody dislikes the same thing and I don't like it either. . . .

Yael

PHILIP: I dislike your strong feelings about what you should be.

LITTLE PRINCE: I dislike the thought that you're "older generation."

SHERSHONSKY: I . . . I . . . I dislike the fact that you hide the truth from yourself.

JANE: I dislike the fact that you let a sense of guilt keep you from feeling what you feel.

ROBERT LEA: I can't think of anything I dislike about you.

SARAH: I dislike that you say you're not pretty, and that's not true.

M: I dislike your *perpetual* smile.

BERNARD: I dislike your talk about your scholastic degrees tonight; it put me off.

BOB: I dislike your feeling that there's a limitation on how much emotional happiness a person can have.

KARI: I dislike the guilt about pleasure.

Robert Lea

ROBERT LEA: Okay, Bernie, baby, sock it to me.

BERNARD: I dislike this bravado, and the whole pose.

BOB: I dislike your aggressiveness which makes you impenetrable.

PHILIP: I dislike your unchanging expression.

LITTLE PRINCE: I dislike your inability to relax with just being hip in something, not hip fully.

YAEL: I dislike that you didn't realize that you were as much at fault in the fight as Bernard. You weren't honest with yourself.

SHERSHONSKY: I dislike your refusal to accept your gentle self.

JANE: I dislike that there's nothing about yourself that you'd like to change, and the fact that you're not entirely honest with yourself.

SARAH: I dislike that you think of Little Prince and Philip as "you people."

M: I dislike your lack of openness with Bernard, your insensitivity to Bernard. You like closed off.

ROBERT LEA: To him. But only to him. Okay.

Bernard

BOB: I dislike what comes across as your style of life: the placing of competition, and the importance of sexual intercourse with women.

KARI: I dislike your rigidity.

PHILIP: I dislike the feeling I get that you don't feel you can really learn anything from me.

LITTLE PRINCE: I dislike what you do with a statement. Like, "Either it will, or it won't, so fuck it."

YAEL: I dislike the feeling that women cannot give you anything but sex.

SHERSHONSKY: I dislike it that you constantly seem to smother your sensitivity and warmth and are unable to take things from people.

JANE: I dislike that you're not proud of your strong points. I think you're sensitive but you don't allow yourself to be.

ROBERT LEA (*sarcastically*): I don't think you should change at all. I think you're perfect.

M: What do you dislike about him?

ROBERT LEA: Everything. Everything. And I think he should stay like that. Don't ever change.

LITTLE PRINCE: Wow!

SARAH: I dislike your shit-collecting, collecting the negatives all the time.

M: I dislike your playing Superman all the time, and I dislike your not being able to accept your passivity.

Little Prince

ROBERT LEA: I dislike your theatricality.

LITTLE PRINCE: I do too.

JANE: I dislike what you do with your anger. Instead of getting angry at the person you're angry at, you try to punish people by withdrawing into yourself.

SHERSHONSKY: I dislike, uh, the constant love you give to everyone.

YAEL: I-I-I dislike the lack of control where I feel it would have been better for you to face a little control over situations.

PHILIP: I dislike your statements sometimes.

KARI: I dislike your mind.

BOB: I dislike your quotations and expressions.

BERNARD: I dislike your preciousness, but your body more than makes up for it.

ROBERT LEA (*to Bernard*): You dislike it that she's not fucking for you!

M: I dislike your poetic vagueness.

SARAH: I dislike it when you say "can't"—sooner than you need to.

Philip

SARAH: I dislike it that I didn't get to know you well enough to know what to say.

ROBERT LEA: I dislike your age. It's a drag.

JANE: I dislike your lack of warmth.

SHERSHONSKY: I don't like it that you don't come through as a defined personality.

YAEL: I-I-I feel somewhat similar.

LITTLE PRINCE: I dislike the fact that I haven't heard a really violent statement from you.

KARI: I dislike your cut-offness, and your arrogance, and not caring about us. You're not struggling with us.

BOB: I dislike your aloofness which can very easily be interpreted as arrogance or condescension.

BERNARD: I dislike your apparent inability to get angry.

M: I dislike your letting me pull your hair. If you hadn't let me, you'd have saved me a feeling of feeling shitty about it.

Jane

SHERSHONSKY: I dislike the fact that you've been helping people a lot of the time and somehow I don't feel I know much about you, and somehow you've hidden yourself.

YAEL: Me, too. I-I-I would like much more to know what bothers you.

LITTLE PRINCE: I dislike not having had the chance to share a greater warmth.

PHILIP: I dislike that you got that feeling about me, that I lack warmth, although it's partly true.

KARI: I dislike your niceness. I mistrust it and dislike it.

BOB: I dislike that you were Number Three in the dominance-submissiveness game.

BERNARD: Where would you rather have her?

BOB: At the back.

BERNARD (to Jane): You're a little bit of a mystery to me. I guess I don't like it and I'm a little angry that you sort of ignored me today.

M: I dislike your hatred for your ass. I really do.

SARAH: I was disappointed that you didn't really take a personal trip.

ROBERT LEA: I dislike that you have a really groovy boyfriend.

Bob

KARI: Oh, I dislike, and feel for, your struggles.

BERNARD: I dislike the fact that now I feel that you are the one who voted against me. Other than that, you're a nice guy.

M: I dislike the fact that you haven't given me anything to dislike about you, that you played it so close.

SARAH: There's a certain inside stiffness which I dislike.

ROBERT LEA: You can't be all that groovy, but I couldn't get involved with you to find something to dislike.

JANE: I dislike the fact that I really think you really are a really "nice guy."

SHERSHONSKY: I dislike that you can't express anger when it's in you.

YAEL: I dislike that you give that image of being stiff.

LITTLE PRINCE: I think I too dislike the fact that you haven't given me something to dislike about you, but I know you could.

PHILIP: All I really dislike is your beard.

Kari

M: I dislike your not looking at people, your vagueness, your not being able to say what you're feeling.

BERNARD: I dislike, but more I feel compassion for, your inability to express your feelings.

BOB: I dislike your silence.

PHILIP: I dislike your hostility.

LITTLE PRINCE: I dislike the fact that you feel you're incapable of your emotions and that you're not doing anything about it. And that you have the same face right now as you did before.

YAEL: I dislike the missing of being able to put into words of what you feel.

SHERSHONSKY: I dislike the anger within you, and your inability to be honest about your emotions.

JANE: I dislike your hatred of yourself, and I also think you hate other people.

ROBERT LEA: I dislike the fact that you're unable to be feminine.
SARAH: I dislike the vagueness.

M

BERNARD: I dislike the fact that you're better-looking than I am, and, uh, in some ways a more effective person.
BOB: I dislike, in a jealous sense, your intellectual ability.
KARI: I dislike your own sense of power to play God under the banner of Good.
LITTLE PRINCE: I dislike that you're not concerned with your beautifulness, and I don't mean physically.
M: I don't understand. You can say it in one short sentence.
LITTLE PRINCE: . . . That beautiful people aren't concerned with their own beautifulness, and that you're that close away, but not quite there yet.
YAEL: I dislike that you are not able to discard a sense of mistrust which you project.
SHERSHONSKY: I dislike that on some occasions you come through a little casual and smart-alecky.
JANE: I dislike your rigidity.
ROBERT LEA: I dislike that you are completely unaware of your fucking opportunism.
SARAH: I like your bluntness, but sometimes I think you're too rough, relating too much like a bulldozer.

SCENE 9: HE LOVES ME

M: Now you'll each sit down in the center again, and everybody will tell you something they like about you.

Kari

KARI: I'd like to hear something somebody likes about me.

M: I think you're very beautiful. I like the way you look as a woman.

BERNARD: I think you're enormously sexy.

BOB: I like what I think is a very keen mind which is a little bit clouded now.

PHILIP: I like that you're sensitive.

LITTLE PRINCE: I like your womanliness, and the fact that you can go a lot further with it.

YAEL: I like your struggle to make something out of something.

SHERSHONSKY: I . . . I like that you're concerned with other people's feelings and would help other people if they need help.

JANE: I like when you let your anger out.

KARI: Gee, that's a comfort, because I'm always afraid people won't like that.

ROBERT LEA: I like the fact that you *could* be sensuous.

SARAH: I like your intensity and your depth. And . . . oh . . . I like you because you didn't take your clothes off! (*Laughter.*)

Jane

BOB: I like the earnestness with which you tried to help various people during the day.

KARI: I like the clarity and simplicity of you.

PHILIP: I like your ability to focus.

LITTLE PRINCE: I like your direct going to the heart of things.

YAEL: I-I-I like you physically first. You're very beautiful, and I like your touch, your clearness. I look at you and I think of some stream coming down in the Alps.

SHERSHONSKY: I like looking at you. I like your smile. I like the clarity with which you express your feelings, and I like that you are really concerned with people.

ROBERT LEA: I like your ability to get involved with people when you want to.

SARAH: I like your forthright assertiveness and warmth.

M: I like your toughness and bluntness.

BERNARD: I guess I like your breasts best.

Yael

SHERSHONSKY: I like the way you have participated, gotten into things which were not in your European background. You tried to break loose.

JANE: I like your liveliness and your willingness to take chances and loosen up.

ROBERT LEA: I like your eagerness to become a part of this whole thing.

SARAH: I like your courage.

M: I like the tragic part of you.

BERNARD: I like the way you took your clothes off.

BOB: I like your spunkiness.

KARI: I like your thrust, and your sense of life and aliveness, and also your sadness which I feel for very much.

PHILIP: I like your openness.

LITTLE PRINCE: I like every big little inch of your fight to live with your tragedy.

Robert Lea

KARI: I like the fact that I picked on you tonight.

PHILIP: I like your mind.

LITTLE PRINCE: I like your ventures into what isn't *only* hip, and what is very good and beautiful.

YAEL: I like that you didn't give in to Kari. I like that you tried very hard.

SHERSHONSKY: I like the way you maintain your façade.

JANE: I like that you dig life and people.

SARAH: I liked the way you approached Kari, and I also like your carriage, and I also like your sturdiness.

M: I like the quickness of your mind.

BERNARD: What I liked most about you tonight was your refusal to be put off by Kari. I . . . I really admire your ability to be rebuffed and, uh . . . not let it deter you.

BOB: I like your wit.

Little Prince

BOB: I hope it doesn't hurt your feelings, but, uh, I like your breasts and your ass best.

BERNARD: I like your breasts.

> *Little Prince begins to sigh deeply with a kind of hopelessness.*

KARI: I also like your body.

PHILIP: I like the way you make me feel. Very good . . . groovy . . .

YAEL: I like your guts in coming back, and I also like your body.

SHERSHONSKY: I like your body.

JANE: I like your body too. And I like your ability to dig things, and I like, when you're happy, the way that you're happy.

ROBERT LEA: I like your body, your face, your mind, and your age. You've got so many wild things in store for you.

LITTLE PRINCE: Good. . . .

SARAH: I like it that you came back, and I also like it that you gave me something.

M: I love the view of your pussy, sitting there with your legs up. (*The group applauds.*) That long, beautiful slit . . . I've been looking at some of the other women too. They don't nearly have the same kind of show. In other circumstances, I could bury my head and stay in there for weeks. And screw T. S. Eliot! (*Laughter.*)

Bob

YAEL: I most like your gentleness and your smile.

SHERSHONSKY: I like the way you stepped into an unfamiliar situation and stepped forth to keep things moving.

YAEL: I second that.

JANE: Yeah, I second that one. And I like just about everything about you, your warmth and your honesty.

ROBERT LEA: I like your gentleness.

SARAH: I like your warmth and the fact that you struggled to get ahead of me for that place in line.

M: I liked the fact that you were the first person to pick out someone to send out of the room.

BERNARD: Yeah. As much as I dislike saying the same things as everybody else, I like your openness, your willingness to assume responsibility for initiating things. I think you're a tremendously straight, decent guy.

KARI: I like that you want to "become."

PHILIP: I like the effort you're making to face yourself.

LITTLE PRINCE: I like your gentle awareness of your ability to begin.

M

JANE: I love the way you look.

ROBERT LEA: I like that I know you.

SARAH: Gee, I like most everything about you.

BERNARD: The quality I admire most is your *chutzpah*. (*Laughter.*)

YAEL: I second Bernard.

BOB: Which in Irish means . . .

ROBERT LEA: . . . balls. Unmitigated gall.

BOB: I think I like the way you asked Little Prince to paint little things on your arms.

KARI: I like your zest for life.

PHILIP: I like that you did this whole thing today.

LITTLE PRINCE: I like that I love you for what you've shown me.

YAEL: I like your looks, and your quick mind and intelligence. I also admire your *chutzpah*.

SHERSHONSKY: I like the gentleness and tender care you showed to two people who were on the floor here and very upset. I was surprised to see that, 'cause that seems so different from all the rest of you.

SARAH: I like your skill.

Philip

SHERSHONSKY: I like your gentleness, and your hands, and the kind of person you're trying to be.

JANE: I like the way you got back into the group.

ROBERT LEA: I like what appears to be your naïveté, and how like a sponge you sucked up this whole day and won't forget it.

SARAH: I like your youth and your looks.

M: I like your telling people to ask you questions.

BERNARD: I like your gentleness.

BOB: I like your hair, and all that represents.

KARI: I like what you don't like about you—such as what comes to your mind first.

LITTLE PRINCE: I like, ergo, your loving warmth in a singular way.

YAEL: I like your gentleness and your youth.

PHILIP: I'm not going to be here too long at this rate! (*Laughter.*)

Sarah

BOB: I like the warmth and sympathy you generate.

KARI: I like your nudeness and your persistence and your struggle.

PHILIP: I like your mind also. I think you're brilliant.

LITTLE PRINCE: I like your sudden, quiet nudeness there in the corner, and the fact that you still like my flower.

YAEL: The thing I like best is your maturity. I had the feeling that very often we said the same thing. You make me feel very good.

SARAH: You too.

SHERSHONSKY: I . . . I . . . like the way your eyes are so extremely expressive, and this quality of a kind of very feminine kind of thing . . . a quiet . . . a very strong feminine quality about you.

JANE: I like your capacity for love and your youth.

ROBERT LEA: I like your sensitivity and your mind.

M: I like your mind and your openness to new experience.

BERNARD: I guess the thing I like most is your tragic quality.

Shershonsky

BERNARD: I like what you're capable of doing, particularly with your hands.

BOB: I like the quiet stability and responsibility.

KARI: I like your needs, and I like you very much.

BERNARD: You like his what?

KARI: His needs.

BERNARD: I thought you said his knees.

PHILIP: I like the way you perceive me.

LITTLE PRINCE: I like your coming loving very much, and your name.

YAEL: I like your very strong sense of manliness and of reliability and of security.

JANE: I like your quest for love.

ROBERT LEA: I like your gentleness, your sensitivity.

SARAH: I like your integrity, and also your looks.

Bernard

BOB: I like your beard.

KARI: I like your stubbornness. (*She laughs.*)

M: You like his stubbornness?

KARI: Yes, I do!

PHILIP: I like your sharpness.

LITTLE PRINCE: I like your stubbornness too, and your liking, come hell or high water, what you're like.

YAEL: I like your mind; also that search for assurance.

SHERSHONSKY: I . . . I . . . admired the way you exposed yourself, and that I learned that there's much more depth to you.

BERNARD (*to Jane*): Don't say you like my breasts.

JANE: I like your ass. I like your stubbornness and your aggressiveness and your openness.

ROBERT LEA: I like your right earlobe. Probably under other circumstances I would have gotten to like you very much.

BERNARD: What other circumstances?

ROBERT LEA: Outside this kind of thing. Here I got to see the part of you I didn't like.

M (*as Robert Lea's alter ego*): "The thing that I dislike in *me.*"

ROBERT LEA: Dislike in me? No.

SARAH: I think what I liked best tonight was your willingness, even though I think it was very hard, to look at what some of your hang-ups were.

M: I like your honesty, and your being able to present the kind of feelings that you're least proud of. I like that in some ways you told more about yourself than I ever would have expected. And I like that you took it all very seriously.

YAEL: Including the votes.

LITTLE PRINCE: Yeah.

PHILIP: *Especially* the votes.

SCENE 10: DISCUSSION

M: Anyone want to say how they felt about the dislike-like thing?

BERNARD: I think there's a general tendency among people to make other people feel good rather than tell them exactly how they feel. And I think this can be irritating.

M: I think that's true. For instance, "You're not telling me that *I'm* as obnoxious as I want you to tell me I am." (*He laughs.*)

PHILIP: But people were trying to be constructive, to help.

SHERSHONSKY: I was surprised how accepting I was of why people disliked me. That was all right. I didn't mind that. But I was disturbed at hearing why people *liked* me.

M: You're uncomfortable telling people you like them, so how can you let them tell you they like *you?*

LITTLE PRINCE: I was a little disturbed at first for people to say they liked my body, and not mention anything else. I would have liked it if somebody said something about me that wasn't physical. But that's okay, and now I enjoy it.

M: I want to say a couple of things. (*He looks at Jane.*) Your comments to me about disliking my rigidity—that kind of blew my mind. I never heard that before from anybody. And I don't feel it's true. . . . And I forgot to mention to you, Robert Lea, that one of the things I disliked about you was that you didn't invite me along on that thing you're going to have with that girl this week. (*Laughter.*) And then when you talked about my opportunism . . . Jeez, I always do what I want to do, or try to . . . but I don't want to see that girl anyway with you because you'd fit it into a bag about my opportunism. So, in retrospect, I'm just as glad you didn't ask me to go with you. . . .

Act 9: The Windup

SCENE 1: WHAT'S IN A NAME?

Slowly, almost unwillingly, the nine nude participants and M begin to reach for their clothes.

M: Now I'd like to know why each of you chose the name you chose. . . .

PHILIP: Why did you pick your name, Shershonsky? Really, why did you? I mean as a single, first name.

SHERSHONSKY: Well . . . my ancestors . . . my grandfather came from Russia to this country, and the family name was Shershonsky. And when they came to this country, they changed that name and made it into a short . . . I don't know, kind of a short Americanized Anglo-Saxon kind of name. And, uh, in recent years I've often had a yearning to be "Shershonsky."

PHILIP: As a last name?

SHERSHONSKY: Well, that's my family name, really. That's the name that came here, and I would like to say to hell with this other name that people use now, and I've often thought of changing my name back to the old one, and that's why I chose it for today.

PHILIP: I . . . I understand that.

SHERSHONSKY (*loudly*): It feels good to hear people call me that! I was never called that in my whole life, and yet that's the name that came to this country on a boat, and now it's gone. . . .

ROBERT LEA (*quietly*): That's very beautiful.

SARAH: Oh, yes. I'm glad you chose that.

YAEL: Yes, Shershonsky, it's very nice, very beautiful, that you chose it.

PHILIP: It's just that I don't like to be called a last name because it's not personal. . . . It's so much easier to, uh . . . (*His voice trails off.*)

SARAH: I like it, but I'm glad you told us why you chose it because for a while I was thinking maybe you chose it so that no one would remember what it was! I chose Sarah because it's a simple name. I like simple names. My own name's a simple name. But I used to dislike my own name, and I used to wish my mother hadn't given it to me. So today, "Sarah" occurred to me.

KARI: "Kari Olsen" is the most common of all Norwegian names. First I was thinking in terms of picking an American name, but then I thought, "No, I don't want to do that"—so I took the most common Norwegian name I could think of.

BOB: I always wished my parents had named me Robert, and for today I took that, and shortened it to "Bob."

BERNARD: I guess I must have felt some identification with the Jules Pfeiffer character "Bernard."

JANE AND SARAH (*in chorus*): But why "Schlossberg?"

BERNARD: I can't explain that.

M: Kind of making fun of yourself? Going with the negative?

SARAH: Well, "Bernard" and "Schlossberg," it's kind of a very good combination, a sort of perfect thing.

YAEL: Do you know what it means—"Schlossberg"? It means *castle,* and a *mountain.*

PHILIP: I sort of like the way "Philip" sounds when you say it.

YAEL: I thought you looked like Philippe Gerard.

ROBERT LEA: Gerard Philippe . . .

PHILIP: I don't really feel like a Philip at all.

ROBERT LEA: You look like a Philip. I chose Robert Lea

I looked through a book yesterday, and it was a nice name, for lack of a better name.

JANE: I chose Jane because it's simple, and I think it's beautiful. I always had this fantasy of always being a famous singer or a famous actress or something like that, and my name is going to be Jane Silver, and I'll always wear silver clothes.

PHILIP: Heigh ho, Silver!

YAEL: At first I wanted to take my own real name that I was called in Europe and am not called here. Then I chose the middle name of my daughter, which I gave her after my father, taking the letters of my father's name and turning them around.

LITTLE PRINCE: After I went through all of e. e. cummings' poetry I decided not to take "Spring." I just thought of Little Prince, and it really turned out to be good, especially when you started calling me "Little Princess." It sort of reversed things. My aunt often called me Little Princess . . . but Little Prince, you know, it had much more meaning to me all night long. I just love Little Prince.

ROBERT LEA: You should call yourself Early Spring.

LITTLE PRINCE (*laughing, blushing*): Early Spring . . . that's two words run together in an e. e. cummings poem.

M: I took M, for Martin, because I liked holding on to a piece of myself. And I like . . . (*he glances at Little Prince mischievously*) . . . the Kafkaesque quality . . . "K" running around, so now "M."

SARAH: There wasn't much point in your taking a pseudonym.

M: No, I guess not. I was wondering whether I should, or whether I shouldn't, and I think, because I knew most of you in some way, I wanted to set a tone of difference, so you wouldn't think I was taking you exactly as I've known you before.

L: Yeah, that was a smart idea. Did you know all of us equally

M: I don't think I knew anybody here well before, except Robert Lea—but I've gotten to know him a lot better here. And I think I kept confusing you, Bob and Philip, because you seemed in my mind to be very much alike in some ways . . . like neither of you are able to say "Cut the shit."

BERNARD: I wanted to ask if, uh, you picked some people who have, uh . . . real psychiatric problems, and some people who don't. Now, did you do this deliberately, or is it just circumstances?

PHILIP: Who do you think has a real psychiatric problem?

BERNARD: That is a tremendously loaded question! Do you think I should go into this now? At two fifteen in the morning?
There is a chorus of yeses.

M: Just say it, Bernard.

BERNARD: Um . . . I think Kari, and I think Little Prince.

M: And who doesn't?

BERNARD: The rest of you are all, uh . . . with the exception of Bob, probably just neurotics.

M: And you?

BERNARD: I forgot about myself. . . . (*He half laughs.*) That's funny that I should not include myself. I suppose I'm somewhere between, uh, normal—

LITTLE PRINCE: You mean healthy.

BERNARD: Uh, between normal and a neurotic person. I'm halfway between them.

M: The truth of the matter is, I talked to everybody I knew about volunteering for this, and the first ten people who said yes, I took. And I was concerned about getting half men and half women. Half the people I talked to wanted to do it. The only person I didn't know before was Little Prince. I spoke to a friend of mine and said, "Listen, I got all these people lined up and I still got one space open for a woman, and I would kind of like to get some young, vibrant thing who might turn

on the men, so we can get into sexual feelings." So he sent
Little Prince. (*Laughter.*)

YAEL: You have never met each other before?

LITTLE PRINCE: No.

YAEL: There I would have lost a hundred-dollar bet.

JANE: When you said half men and half women just now, it was
the first time I realized that all day I had the feeling that there
were more men.

M: Well, there's me. But then again, there's Marjorie out there,
which equalizes.

BERNARD: Well, I was just interested in an answer to my question about choosing for psychiatric—

M: Listen, Bernard, I want to tell you, for what it's worth, that
I think you're just as hung-up, you know, as the worst person
here who's hung-up.

PHILIP: But there's nothing wrong with that.

M: There's nothing wrong with it. Right.

LITTLE PRINCE: It's okay.

SCENE 2: WHAT DO YOU DO?

M: Someone, before, said they wanted to know what people did.
I'm a psychiatrist. (*Laughter.*)

YAEL (*shouting*): I'm guessing Bernard is a sociologist, without
a final degree!

PHILIP: Bernard's a businessman.

BOB: He's a commercial artist.

JANE: He's a biologist!

ROBERT LEA: I think he's a chemist without a PhD.

People begin to talk and shout, cutting each other off.

BERNARD: I'm a research pathologist.

JANE: What's a pathologist?

M: It's a doctor who works with dead people and examines tissues.

THE GROUP (*again overlapping*): You're an M.D.? An M.D.? You work with dead bodies?

BERNARD: I don't work with dead people.

YAEL: Did you ever study sociology?

BERNARD: I was once very interested in going into psychiatry, but, uh . . . I didn't.

KARI: Sarah, what do you do?

SARAH: I'm a psychologist and a psychoanalyst.

YAEL: Well! I would never have guessed you're a psychologist! And that's a big compliment to you! You are too sensitive for being a psychologist!

M: You're not up-tight enough for being a psychologist.

YAEL (*incredulously*): I would never have . . . I would never . . .

SARAH (*laughing*): I'm proud for myself, and I'm insulted for my profession.

KARI: Philip, what do you do?

PHILIP: I study psychology, and I'm a motorcycle messenger on the side.

SHERSHONSKY: Uh . . . uh, I'm a sculptor, but I don't, uh—

BERNARD: He's a very talented sculptor, too.

SHERSHONSKY: I don't . . . uh, I don't make enough money to work at it. I have another job. . . .

KARI: What is that job?

SHERSHONSKY: Vocational counselor. But, you know . . . sculpting is my thing.

ROBERT LEA: You're going to make it, Shershonsky.

YAEL: You sculpt small sculptures? Or big ones?

SHERSHONSKY: They're getting bigger because I'm feeling bigger inside myself now, I'm thinking bigger.

JANE: I'm an administrative assistant for a youth center on the Lower East Side.

ROBERT LEA: I work with very bright high school students. I teach English in a special class.

M (*playing Bernard's alter ego*): "Special classes eat shit!" (*Then, to Bernard, seriously:*) Do his pupils look all right to you, doctor?

ROBERT LEA: Yeah, check me out, will you?

JANE (*elaborating on the pun*): You mean they're too bright?

BERNARD (*examining Robert Lea's eyes*): No, they're all right.

ROBERT LEA: They're okay?

M AND BERNARD: Yeah, yeah. Okay.

M: Do you feel good?

ROBERT LEA: Yeah. Uh, no. I mean I got hurt here. (*He points to the injured spot on his head.*)

BERNARD (*slowly*): Oh . . . oh . . . *that's* what you were referring to.

YAEL: What does Kari do?

KARI: I'm a mother of two, and an actress.

BERNARD: Little Prince?

LITTLE PRINCE: For money I do anything from teaching to modeling to acting to working with kids. What I'm really doing is working with a psychotherapist—learning about rational living.

KARI: I'm also a carpenter.

JANE (*in disbelief*): A carpenter?

KARI: A carpenter.

BOB: I'm a community organizer, organizing cooperatives on the Lower East Side. Mobilization for Youth.

YAEL: Do you work for an agency, Sarah?

SARAH: No. I have a private practice. What did you think I was?

YAEL: I could have sworn a sociologist.

BOB: I would have said some sort of counselor, vocational, or guidance.

JANE: Or professor.
SHERSHONSKY: Or an administrator at a college.
KARI: And Yael—what do you do?
YAEL: I'm a sociologist.

SCENE 3: ANYONE WALKING OVER TO
         BROADWAY?

*Everyone is dressed. There is a general milling about.
People stand in couples, in odd-number groups, munching last sandwiches, speaking to each other in casual,
friendly tones. There is the quality of the tag end of a
cocktail party. Bernard is overheard apologizing to Little
Prince for naming her one of the two possible "psychiatric cases." She reassures him that she was not hurt by it.
Marty asks for help in cleaning things up. Several people
volunteer and begin to put away food and to tidy up the
office, the foyer, and the kitchen.
There are other personal comments: "I'm glad . . . ,"
"I liked . . . ," and "You're beautiful. . . ."
Then Robert Lea bounds back into the room, full of
life, smiling, loud, bosom buddy to the group and to the
world. . . .*
ROBERT LEA: Anyone walking over to Broadway?

The tape ends.

PART TWO

EVALUATION

1. Marathon Observed

Marjorie Lee

Five months have elapsed between the enactment of *Marathon 16* and this writing; but I might have met its ten participants this morning. They're still clear. They're still a breathing part of me. Usually, I find it hard to contemplate the meaning of masses. I don't belong to clubs. I'm person- rather than people-oriented and cope best with one-to-one relationships. Yet I find myself, for the first time in my life, *in love with a group*. I mean that literally. In the past five months, I've had all the symptoms: moments of joy in remembering, mixed with moments of that strange yearning and sadness which are so intrinsic to the in-love syndrome. I want these people back together again, where I can see them and hear them and smell the body musk which permeated that small room—all of them: the ones whom I found beautiful and thrilling, *and* the ones who irritated the hell out of me. I've thought at times of telephoning one or another of them. But I haven't. Because what I've just said is true: my in-loveness is with the group. These ten individuals form one entity.

This has happened before, to other people. In September, 1969, I attended, as a participant, a demonstration mini-marathon led by William Schutz. At the end of the evening he asked for reactions from several of many five-people teams. And then he announced: "That group over there in the corner has decided to get married." That's the feeling. I'd marry the *Marathon 16* bunch if I could.

I can't, on more levels than one. To begin with, *they* don't know *me*. So, in terms of love, I'm in the position of the grimy little kid standing with her face pressed against the candy-store window.

My isolation from June 21 at 10 A.M. until June 22 at approximately 2:30 A.M. was a new and painful experience. There were rough moments when it played on the sore spots of my unconscious mind and drummed up the inner sounds of paranoia. Within a day or so, when I had slept off my fatigue and settled back to stability, I came to a strong realization: Isolation is too high a price to pay for safety. To be placed high on a mountain, out of the reach of any battle raging below, would be far more difficult than joining in and facing the danger.

Not that my mountain gave me emotional immunity. I saw Sarah's beauty as a woman, and responded to it. I wept, unseen, for Kari and Little Prince. I found Bernard fascinating and couldn't forget for a minute that, for me, he was the man with the most sex appeal. I was aware that Jane was rather like me in her straight approach to things, and, because of that likeness, less interesting to me than the other women. I knew that Robert Lea was a man I had often met before, in other guises, and with whom I could rap for nights on end in many intellectual areas. I had to fight down my anger at the stumbling, hesitant passivity of Bob and Philip and Shershonsky. "Not my kind of men," I kept telling myself with a subjectivity shameful in any supposedly objective reporter. Yet, several months later I met Shershonsky at the Schutz demonstration and his very "niceness" turned me on. And Yael? *Courage*—that old word *courage*. It was so strong in her that it came through to me like a great slap of high wind. When, in about the twelfth hour, I felt I might pass out, I needed only to look at her to stay alert. When you're near someone with a Hitler-blighted childhood, you don't tell yourself that sixteen hours of silent note-taking is "too tiring."

One of the most interesting things about my nonparticipatory experience was the viewing, in actuality, of the Acting-Out Technique. As a tried and true analysand of the Freudian school, I lived my long years on the couch in the deep belief that, as my analyst put it over and over again, "We are here to analyze; we do not act out." We were; and we didn't. Cut loose from therapy with an acceptably honorable discharge, I went back in and proceeded to analyze some more. To watch the "do-ings" of *Marathon 16* was something else again: People were being instructed to practice, to live overtly. Physicality, while not a total replacement for thinking, was certainly an adjunct to it. While the symbolic womb had at some time or another affected all these people, they were encouraged to leave it for life experience. Bernard and Jane had "never before" believed that they could expose their bodies in a group situation. Ber-nard had "never before" kissed a pretty girl on impulse. Bob had "never before" accepted his masturbation, which, when shared physically with strangers, proved to be acceptable after all.

It was my observation of *Marathon 16* which prompted me to participate in the Schutz demonstration two and a half months later, to look into the much-disputed theories of Albert Ellis, and to emerge with the feeling that marathon-encounter methods are an essential *second half* of therapy—a natural and needed continuation for traditional analysis. I found nothing in either experience, nor in Ellis' book on Rational Living, which could not in one way or another be traced back and related to Freud. It is the technique which differs; and in that new tech-nique lies the opportunity to put self-understanding to produc-tive and constructive use. To link the new-wave therapists with old Dr. Freud is to arouse their anger; yet I find I must, if only insofar as basic therapeutic goals are concerned. The traditionalists want you to *feel* your freedom; the new-wavers want you to *live* it. And of the shock of this concept to the old guard it can only be said that Freud himself would be shocked as well—by the dogmatic refusal of his followers to go forward, to change, and to build new concepts more fitting to a new world.

A major question: Will the effects on participants of marathon therapy last? The answer is the same as that which is given by Ellis for the potential success of RET (Rational-Emotive Therapy.) *"Work on it, forever, by yourself."* And as I recall, my traditional analyst came through with the same thought: "I'm giving you the analytic tools. When you leave here, use them." She meant, however, for me to use them emotionally, and to think of what I had learned, and to *feel* a new way. It isn't enough. There has got to be the trial and error, and the trial and non-error, of *doing*. I don't change because I know that my mother was the initial cause of my agoraphobia. *I must enter crowds.*

As witness to *Marathon 16* I saw fear, discomfort, and self-doubt on full display. And then, as the hours wore on, the slow evaporation of them. Unfortunately, Sarah, with her body consciousness, along with Kari and her even greater rigidity, were the two participants to remain frozen in premarathon concepts. But it is important to consider the time gap between experience and realization of experience—a gap which occurs in any form of therapy. Often, following psychoanalysis, years pass before the ex-analysand discovers the gains. They have simply been there, lying dormant in the unconscious, waiting to burst into awareness.

The word *unconscious* appears rather low on the terminology lists of a good many new-wave therapists. Yet again, I find that to be a sidestepping of basic issues. It's all right with me if you want to call something "unawareness" or "out of awareness." It *means* "the unconscious"—and to quibble with Freud on a semantic level strikes me as nit-picking.

Sarah, then, and Kari may find at any moment, on any day, or in any year, that the inner bans on body exposure have lifted within them. For Kari, the realization may pass unnoticed. For Sarah, a professional in the field, the change will be met consciously. The chances are good for her. The hang-up, in spite of various rationalizations given by her to the group, was related mostly to her breasts, which are in fact quite beautiful in that they evince her experience as a woman. For me, the perfection of Little Prince's body was less beautiful for the lack of just that experience.

If I seem to dwell on this, it's because I identify. After the birth and care of my five children, and the number of years spent loving and being loved, my own breasts show the same signs of use. I, too, felt self-conscious about them, and yearned for a replay of my youth. Then I forced myself into a breast-baring encounter with my collaborator, and within three minutes my self-doubts were dispelled. The importance—the neurotic, joy-killing *importance*—we place on our physical selves! Idiots that we are, swayed by the dictates of our particular country, we begin to believe that we would trade in the whole marvelous issue of mature womanhood for two small up-tilted nipples!

But we learn. Painfully, we learn. And much of what was learned, through active effort and experiment, is seeding quietly in the dark corners of our participants' psyches.

And what was learned, really? I would rather deal, as would Jane, in basics now, skipping the individual purposes of M's eight procedures and their various subcategories. At bottom, he was working with, and upon, fear. We can list a thousand human hang-ups by name, but only one fundamental motivation: fear.

"It's bad!"

"It's not right!"

"Nobody does, or ever will, love me!"

And from this stem hatred and prejudice against others. No, prejudice isn't a question of "narrow-mindedness." It is simply the symptom of an illness called Fear . . . an illness which can't be cured by medicine, drugs, *or* mere understanding. In the past the deliberate plunge into a fearful or seemingly danger-ous situation was called "counterphobic action"—and it was frowned upon by classicists. A mistake, I feel. It's only by taking that plunge that we will ever discover the unreality of most of our fears. And only then will we who are Bernard cease to take popularity polls and end our quests for ephemeral "normalcy"; and those of us who are Shershonsky or Bob, reap the rewards of saying "I love you"; and those of us who are Sarah, realize that loneliness is self-imposed; and those of us who are Robert Lea, stop hiding our true gentleness; and those of us who are a composite of all our ten participants, walk on the streets of this vast, crazy world as Yael did later: straighter, and with the free-dom of a bounce.

2. Commentary

Martin Shepard, M.D.

Traditional psychiatric concepts, based on a medical model, presumed patients to suffer from a sickness: a disease that could be cured by discovering its pathological origins and understanding them. The even earlier concern with proper diagnoses of various subspecies of schizophrenia and neurosis led to a search for dietary, genetic, and chemical factors, in the hope of finding a cure. Freud's psychoanalytic theories embodied similar thinking. Just as skin infections must be drawn to a head and lanced in order to be cured, so were the causes of trauma in childhood searched out, recaptured, and relieved. However, these ideas failed to account for numerous individuals who had undergone the same sorts of traumas without exhibiting the troublesome symptoms shown by those people who labeled themselves "patients."

A proper appreciation of the marathon necessitates a shift in perspective from the traditional ways in which psychological groups have been viewed. To see this group as one composed of *sick people in need of therapy* is not only to miss the point but also to do damage to a wider conception of what human beings are all about.

It has proved far more useful for many—including myself— to account for psychological "illness" not in terms of malignant factors but rather in terms of *absent* ones. For a variety of reasons all of us fail to take varying quantities of world or societal data into our comprehensions. For most of us, this failure to take in and synthesize new experiences and knowledge leads to a deadening existence: the boring, humdrum routine of sameness. For a few, this failure to keep gaining in awareness is positively crippling; and from this defect stem all manner of social maladaptions known as *symptoms*.

From birth we are continually offered new data from our interactions with the world. If a person is to continue to grow psychologically as well as physically, new information and conceptions will continue to register until the moment of death. Thus, we are never fully realized until we die.

Adopting this viewpoint, it can be seen that from "sickest" to "healthiest" we all suffer, necessarily, from the same phenomenology: that of incomplete awareness. Those who are fortunate have eyes that can see, ears that can hear, hands that can touch, and souls that dare to upset their current equilibriums. They are thus in a position continually to integrate new material from life. They know that every human being grows his own brain, and they can nourish and enjoy their awareness as their interests strike them. Most of us, however, are taught from infancy on that there are certain questions not to ask, certain things not to say, certain actions not to take, and certain ideas not even to consider. These prohibitions, supposedly necessary for "socialization," are usually not necessary at all in order to rear responsible adult human beings. More often than not the result is similar to that of poorly housebroken puppies: When the "master" is watching you, you deposit your excreta in an appropriate place; but when he is away, anything can and will be soiled.

While our school systems attempt to teach children to relate to spelling, mathematics, and geography, there is no real effort made to teach people how they relate to each other. I am sure that much of the interest in encounter groups today stems from the fact that such "courses" in human interaction were missing in our educational processes. These intensive group meetings are thus educational in the broadest sense. One does not have to be sick to partake of them; only curious. Formal psychotherapy itself makes a great leap forward when it embraces the concept that it is simply a part of the process of higher education.

The marathon experience is thus one that attempts to create a climate in which accelerated learning is possible. The unasked questions are asked, the forbidden actions are risked, and the formerly unhearing ears are fed new information. If the participant leaves such new ways of relating behind when he leaves the marathon, he has experienced little more than a "turn-on." On the other hand, those who continue the process receive an emotional payoff which continues to foster further growth.

One of my most rewarding experiences resulting from *Marathon 16* occurred a month later when I met Shershonsky socially. He was telling how the marathon had altered his life. He illustrated by relating an incident which occurred in a cafeteria. He was talking to an acquaintance when he noticed mucus discharging from his friend's nostril. Said Shershonsky, "So I told him, 'Hey, you've got snot coming out of your nose.' Now that may not mean much to you," he added animatedly, "but I would never in my life have even thought of saying such a thing before to anyone. And it felt great to be able to have that freedom." It was also Shershonsky who, several days after his *Marathon 16* experiences, called his traditional psychoanalyst by her first name, planted a fond kiss on her cheek, and terminated his therapy on the basis of his new freedom to be himself.

As for marathon and encounter leaders: I conceive this task to be one of creating a climate of openness and learning. Some of the ways with which to accomplish this are obvious in the structure of *Marathon 16*. Various procedures were aimed at bringing to light heretofore little-discussed experiences (The Most Shameful Thing, The Most Distressing Thing). Others encouraged risk-taking in order to allow participants to see more vividly how they often, and unnecessarily, limit themselves. At times nonverbal exercises helped to eliminate the self-deceptions that speech so often gives rise to. Other procedures often considered "asocial" (Nudity, Take a Walk, He Loves Me—He Loves Me Not) allowed exploration of bodily misconceptions and the universality of the love-hate relationship.

Creation of this open climate means that the leader must be willing to become a transparent self, volunteering his own experiences when he thinks this might be helpful and showing the same willingness to respond to questioning that he asks of the other participants.

Finally, he must try to foster an atmosphere of ultimate helpfulness as opposed to allowing members of the group merely to engage in name-calling. Guided fantasies and the Gestalt method of encouraging people to role-play their conflicts are particularly useful in getting them into themselves instead of into interpretive disputes with other participants. Helpfulness also occurs when you can vividly demonstrate to someone ways in which his present life style opposes additional satisfactions otherwise available.

I don't believe a leader need wait quietly to analyze the source of "pathology." Rather, it seems more fruitful to encourage participants to explore new possibilities of interaction (for Sarah more actively to pursue her wishes; for Bernard more passively to pursue his) and to help people realize they are Everyman when it comes to certain areas of shame and doubt (Bob's masturbation).

That *we are all in this world together* is another invaluable potential experience available in a marathon encounter. We can easily see the need to have the crew of a spaceship treat each other rationally and fairly, to recycle waste products so as not to poison their limited environment, to avoid the pettiness, jealousies, envies, and hatreds practiced so prolifically on Earth. And yet Earth is just such a space capsule in the vacuum of the universe. The material and interpersonal pollution engaged in here is every bit as dangerous to the survival of the species.

If experiences such as the marathon can do no more than heighten this sense of human interrelatedness and can lead to the conclusion that we are all ultimately responsible for ourselves and accountable for what we do to others, they will continue to play some small but useful part in the perpetuation of mankind.